BRIGHT NOTES

RICHARD III
BY
WILLIAM
SHAKESPEARE

Intelligent Education

Nashville, Tennessee

BRIGHT NOTES: Richard III
www.BrightNotes.com

No part of this publication may be used or reproduced in any manner whatsoever without written permission, except in the case of brief quotations in critical articles and reviews. For permissions, contact Influence Publishers http://www.influencepublishers.com.

ISBN: 978-1-645425-80-9 (Paperback)
ISBN: 978-1-645425-81-6 (eBook)

Published in accordance with the U.S. Copyright Office Orphan Works and Mass Digitization report of the register of copyrights, June 2015.

Originally published by Monarch Press.
Elizabeth M. Nugent; W. John Campbell, 1964
2020 Edition published by Influence Publishers.

Interior design by Lapiz Digital Services. Cover Design by Thinkpen Designs.

Printed in the United States of America.

Library of Congress Cataloging-in-Publication Data forthcoming.
Names: Intelligent Education
Title: BRIGHT NOTES: Richard III
Subject: STU004000 STUDY AIDS / Book Notes

CONTENTS

1) Introduction to William Shakespeare   1

2) Introduction to Richard III   6

3) Textual Analysis
    Act I   10
    Act II   29
    Act III   41
    Act IV   63
    Act V   84

4) Character Analyses   98

5) Critical Commentary   111

6) Essay Questions and Answers   117

7) Bibliography and Suggestions for Research Papers   128

8) General Biography and Criticism   131

INTRODUCTION TO WILLIAM SHAKESPEARE

On April 26, 1564, William Shakespeare, son of John Shakespeare and Mary Arden, was christened in Holy Trinity Church, Stratford-on-Avon. His birthday is traditionally placed three days before. He was the eldest of four boys and two girls born to his father, a well-to-do glover and trader, who also held some minor offices in the town government. He probably attended the local free school, where he picked up the "small Latin and less Greek" that Ben Jonson credits him with. ("Small" Latin to that knowledgeable classicist meant considerably more than it does today.) As far as is known, this was the extent of Shakespeare's formal education. In November of 1582, when he was eighteen, a license was issued for his marriage to Ann Hathaway, a Stratford neighbor eight years older than himself. The following May their child Susanna was christened in the same church as her father. While it may be inferred from this that his marriage was a forced one, such an inference is not necessary; engagement at that time was a legally binding contract and was sometimes construed as allowing conjugal rights. Their union produced two more children, twins Judith and Hamnet, christened in February, 1585. Shortly thereafter Shakespeare left Stratford for a career in London. What he did during these years - until we pick him up, an established playwright, in 1592 - we do not know, as no records exist. It is presumed that he served an apprenticeship in the theatre, perhaps as a provincial trouper, and eventually won himself a place as an actor. By 1594 he was a successful dramatist with the Lord Chamberlain's company (acting groups had noble protection and patronage), having produced the *Comedy of Errors* and the *Henry VI* trilogy, probably in collaboration with older, better established dramatists. When the plague closed the London theatres for many months of 1593-94, he found himself without a livelihood. He promptly turned his hand to poetry (although written in verse, plays were not considered as dignified as poetry), writing two long narrative poems, *Venus and Adonis* and *The Rape of Lucrece*. He dedicated them to the Earl of Southampton, undoubtedly receiving some recompense. The early nineties also saw the first of Shakespeare's **sonnets** circulating in manuscript, and later finding their way into print. In his early plays - mostly chronicle histories glorifying England's past, and light comedies - Shakespeare sought for popular success and achieved it. In 1599 he was able to buy a share in the Globe Theatre, where he acted and where his plays were performed. His ever-increasing financial success enabled him to buy a good deal of real estate in his native Stratford, and by 1605 he was able to retire from acting. Shortly thereafter he began to spend most of his time in Stratford, to which he retired around 1610. Very little is known of his life after he left London. He died on April 23, 1616, in Stratford, and was buried there. In 1623 the *First Folio* edition of his complete works was published by a group of his friends as a testimonial to his memory. This was a very rare tribute, because at the time plays were generally considered to be inferior literature, not really worthy of publication. These scanty facts, together with some information about the dates of his plays, are all that is definitely known about the greatest writer in the history of English literature. The age in which Shakespeare lived was not as concerned with keeping accurate records as we are, and any further details about Shakespeare's life have been derived from educated guesses based on knowledge of his time. Shakespeare's plays fall into three major groups according to the periods in his development when he wrote them:

EARLY COMEDIES AND HISTORIES

The first group consists of romantic comedies such as *A Midsummer Night's Dream* (1593-5), and of strongly patriotic histories such as *Henry V* (1599). The early comedies are full of farce and slapstick, as well as exuberant poetry. Their plots are complicated and generally revolve around a young love relationship. The histories are typical of the robust, adventurous English patriotism of the Elizabethan era, when England had achieved a position of world dominance and power.

THE GREAT TRAGEDIES

The second period, beginning with *Hamlet* and ending with *Antony and Cleopatra*, is the period of the great tragedies: *Hamlet* (1602); *Othello* (1604); *King Lear* (1605); *Macbeth* (1606); and *Antony and Cleopatra* (1607-8). Shakespeare seems to have gone through a mental crisis at this time. His vision of the world darkens, and he sees life as an **epic** battle between the forces of good and evil, between order and chaos within man and in the whole universe. The forces for good win out in the end over evil, which is self-defeating. But the victory of the good is at great cost and often comes at the point of death. It is a moral victory, not a material one. These tragedies center on a great man who, because of some flaw in his makeup, or some error he commits, brings death and destruction down upon himself and those around him. They are generally considered the greatest of Shakespeare's plays.

THE LATE ROMANCES

In the third period Shakespeare returns to romantic comedy. But such plays as *Cymbeline* (1609-10), *The Winter's Tale* (1610-11), and *The Tempest* (1611) are very different in point of view and structure from such earlier comedies as *Much Ado About Nothing* (1599) and *Twelfth Night* (1600). Each of these late romances has a situation potentially tragic, and there is much bitterness in them. Thus the destructive force of insane jealousy serves as the **theme** both of the tragedy, *Othello*, and the comedy, *The Winter's Tale*. They are serious comedies, replacing farce and slapstick with rich symbolism and supernatural events. They deal with such **themes** as sin and redemption, death and rebirth, and the conflict between nature and society, rather than with simple romantic love. In a sense they are deeply religious, although unconnected with any church dogma. In his last play, *The Tempest*, Shakespeare achieved a more or less serene outlook upon the world after the storm and stress of his great tragedies and the so-called "dark comedies."

SHAKESPEARE'S THEATRE

Shakespeare's plays were written for a stage very different from our own. Women, for instance, were not allowed to act; so female parts, even that of Cleopatra, were played by boy actors whose voices had not yet changed. The plays were performed on a long platform surrounded by a circular, unroofed theatre, and were dependent on natural daylight for lighting. There was no curtain separating the stage from the audience, nor were there act divisions. These were added to the plays by later editors. Because the stage jutted right into the audience, Shakespeare was able to achieve a greater intimacy with his spectators than modern playwrights can. The audience in the pit, immediately surrounding the stage, had to stand crowded together throughout the play. Its members tended to be lower class Londoners who would frequently comment aloud on the action of the play and break into fights. Anyone who attended the plays in the pit did so at the risk of having his pockets picked, of catching a disease, or, at best, of being jostled about by the crude "groundlings." The aristocratic and merchant classes, who watched the plays from seats in the galleries, were spared most of the physical discomforts of the pit.

ITS ADVANTAGES

There were certain advantages, however, to such a theatre. Because complicated scenic, lighting and sound effects were impossible, the playwright had to rely on the power of his words to create scenes in the audience's imagination. The rapid changes of scene and vast distances involved in *Antony and Cleopatra*, for instance, although they create a problem for modern producers, did not for Shakespeare. Shakespeare did not rely - as the modern realistic theatre does - on elaborate stage scenery to create atmosphere and locale. For these, as for battle scenes involving large numbers of people, Shakespeare relied on the suggestive power of his poetry to quicken the imagination of his audience. Elizabethan audiences were very lively anyway, and quick to catch any kind of word play. Puns, jokes, and subtle poetic effects made a greater impression on them than on modern audiences, who are less alert to language.

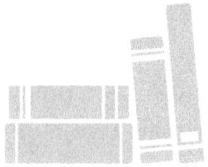

INTRODUCTION TO RICHARD III

SHAKESPEARE

King Richard The Third was probably written in 1592, ten years after Shakespeare had come up to London from Stratford-on-Avon. The playwright was born in that Warwickshire town on April 23, 1564. There is a record that his parents, John Shakespeare and Mary Arden, had him baptized on April 26. It is probable that he attended the town's free grammar school where he used the famous Lily Grammar to which he refers in several of his plays. His attendance at this school was his only formal education. But the grammar schools of his day had a highly developed curriculum so that the boys came out of them with a good smattering of the best ancient and modern Latin authors. In Shakespeare's plays there is evidence that he had read, together with the works of Caesar, Livy, and Sallust, also the plays of Plautus. Terence, and the Mantuan poems. Most likely he had used translations, as he did for Ovid. This would bear out Ben Jonson's comment that Shakespeare knew "little Latin and less Greek." Could Ovid's line, "rudis indigestaque moles," have prompted Lady Anne's description of Richard as a "foul indigested lump?"

KING RICHARD THE THIRD

This early play is perhaps Shakespeare's greatest tribute to Christopher Marlowe. There are the same Marlovian forces at work: a heroic figure meeting his fate after long and violent struggle with opposing forces. In *Richard III*, the use of **blank verse** gives promise of equalling that of Marlowe, though Shakespeare actually surpasses him in the poetry of *Hamlet* and his other great tragic plays.

SOURCES OF KING RICHARD THE THIRD

Controversy has surrounded the exact historical sources which Shakespeare used for this play. He had several to choose from: among the earliest is Sir Thomas More's *The History of King Richard The Third*, written about 1513. It is most probable that More's *History* served as a source for Holinshed's the Union of the two noble and illustre families of Lancaster and Yorke (1550) and Polydore Vergil's *Historia Angliae* (1555). Holinshed's *The Union*, reflects the despotic character that More gives Richard. And More's History is said to come largely from a personal account given him by John Morton, Bishop of Ely, in whose house More lived as a student. The Bishop is a character in the play. In both Hall and Vergil there are strong reflections of More's portrait of Richard. As does More each chronicler points out the evils that spring from misgovernment. Previous to Shakespeare's play a Latin play, *Richardus Tertius* by Dr. Thomas Legge, was performed at St. John's College, Cambridge in 1579. Another play, *The True Tragedie of Richard III* was published in 1594. The first play seems to have had no influence on Shakespeare, but there is a dispute whether or not he used *The True Tragedie*.

BRIEF SUMMARY OF THE PLAY

In 1477 when the House of Lancaster was nearly extinct and no longer a threat to the Yorkists, Richard, Duke of Gloucester (third son of the deceased Richard, Duke of York), is ambitious to become King of England after the death of his sickly brother King Edward IV. His rightful successor is George, Duke of Clarence, the second son. Richard decides to dispose of him and has him murdered in the Tower. In a few years after the murder of Clarence, Edward dies. His last act was an attempt to reconcile his Queen and her family with Richard and his friends at court. At Edward's death, Richard is appointed Royal Protector for Edward's two young sons, Edward, Prince of Wales, and Richard, Duke of York.

In his scheme to gain the Crown, Richard separates the children from their mother Queen Elizabeth and her family, Rivers, Grey, and Vaughan. He finds grounds to accuse Rivers and the others of treason and has them beheaded. When Lord Hastings refuses to agree to setting aside Edward's children in favor of Richard, he is accused of treason and witchcraft at a meeting of the Council and Richard orders him immediately beheaded.

It is through his powerful ally the Duke of Buckingham that public opinion is swayed in favor of Richard. Buckingham gives a public harangue praising Richard and starts a rumor that his late brother, the King, was a bastard son, so that his young sons are illegitimate and not eligible for the Crown. Gathering a large group of citizens led by the Lord Mayor and his train, Buckingham "pleads" with Richard to address them. He pretends his disinterest in being king, but is finally "persuaded" to accept the Crown. He had already imprisoned Edward's sons in the Tower, and shortly after he is crowned King he has them murdered.

To strengthen his hold on the Crown, Richard determines to marry his brother Edward's daughter, Elizabeth. He sends out rumors that his wife Anne is gravely ill. She dies shortly, possibly from poisoning. When Buckingham demurs about murdering Edward's children, Richard is suspicious of him and refuses to fulfill the promises he had given to make him Earl of Hereford and present him with valuables left by his brother Edward. Angered by this treatment, Buckingham raises an army to fight against Richard. He is captured and beheaded.

When things seem triumphant for Richard his hold on the Crown is threatened by the exiled young Duke of Richmond, a stepson of Richard's Lord Chamberlain, Lord Stanley. With the good of the nation at heart, Stanley dupes Richard into thinking he is a loyal supporter. With his great wealth Stanley is able to raise an army and at a crucial moment sends his forces to aid Richmond in the decisive battle of Bosworth Field.

Even after his horse has been killed Richard courageously continues fighting in the battle. In a duel with Richmond he is stabbed to death. His Crown is placed on Richmond's head, who as King becomes Henry VII. He marries Elizabeth, daughter of Edward, whom Richard had vainly sought to marry. Richmond promises peace to the nation with the union of the White and the Red Rose of the Houses of York and Lancaster.

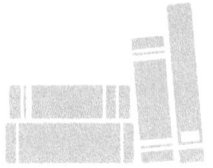

RICHARD III

TEXTUAL ANALYSIS

ACT I

ACT 1: SCENE 1

According to history the play covers about fourteen years-from the death of Henry VI, the last of the Lancastrians, in 1471, to the death of the Yorkist, Richard III, formerly Duke of Gloucester, in 1485. The latter's elder brother, King Edward IV, usurped the throne from Henry VI and reigned until 1483. But for dramatic purposes Shakespeare has crowded the events of these years into a few months.

When the play opens, Richard, Duke of Gloucester, is walking along a London street. He is musing on the peaceful times that have followed the Civil War between the House of Lancaster and the House of York.

Comment

Richard, youngest son of Richard Plantagenet, Duke of York, is responsible for this momentary lull. He helped his brother, Edward, now reigning as Edward IV, seize the throne from the Lancastrian King Henry VI and his son, Edward, Prince of Wales, at the battle of Mortimer's Cross, in 1461. Both were murdered by Richard. (Compare Shakespeare's *King Henry VI*, Act. V. scs. 5 and 7)

Richard's thoughts turn to his ambitions to be King. It will take more bloody work and he is eager for it. Before the play opens he has determined to create hatred between his brothers, King Edward IV and George, Duke of Clarence. He has invented a prophecy and had it relayed to the King. It mentioned a traitor and assassin whose initial is "G". As Richard muses, he admits his villainy is prompted by his deformity - he is a hunchback and lame. He is so ugly that even the dogs on the street bark at him. Since he "cannot prove a lover" he is "determined to be a villain."

Comment

As an arch villain, Richard completely dominates the play and shifts the characters one against the other with ruthless, sardonic humor. In the long opening soliloquy we see the workings of his warped mind and how immune he keeps himself toward the moral consequences of crime.

His thoughts are interrupted by the Duke of Clarence who walks toward him on his way to the Tower. Richard pretends surprise that Clarence has an armed guard. He is pleased at his brother's answer - the fault of the King's belief in an old prophecy given him by a fortune teller. The prophecy portends that the King's life is endangered by a person whose name begins with the letter "G". As the Duke's full name is George, Duke of Clarence, the King will feel more secure if his brother is imprisoned in the Tower. Richard insists that his imprisonment is not the King's doing, but that the King's wife, Lady Elizabeth Grey, and her family are to blame. (Compare Comment Act I, sc. 3) He is supposedly sympathetic with Clarence, and advises him that as things are in the Kingdom both are in danger. They had best keep the King's favor and the Queen's. Most especially he recommends keeping in favor with the King's friend, Mistress Jane Shore. He mentions how she has just obtained Lord Hastings' release from the Tower and may do the same for him. As the brothers part, Richard falsely promises Clarence to work for his release or take his place in the Tower.

Comment

The conversation between the brothers reveals the hypocritical side of Richard. For example, when the two guards interrupt and demand their prisoner move on, Richard seizes the chance to declare his loyalty to the Crown. (The guards would certainly repeat whatever he said to the King.) He chides them that he has spoken no treason. He has praises for everyone, certainly the King, the Queen, and Mistress Shore's "pretty foot." He quips about the guard and her. The scene affords another glimpse of Richard's sardonic humor when he remarks, as Clarence is led away: "Simple, plain Clarence! I do love thee so That I will shortly send thy soul to heaven."

Before Clarence is out of sight Lord Hastings, just released from the Tower, enters. He is greeted by Richard who pretends his distress over sending such worthy subjects as Clarence and Hastings to the Tower while lesser subjects remain free.

Hastings has news of the King's health. He "is sickly, weak and melancholy." Richard, swearing with his usual oath "By Saint Paul," pretends that he is greatly grieved at hearing such bad news. He bids Hastings a hurried farewell. The news of the King's illness disturbs him since the King may die before Clarence. Clarence must die before the King! Otherwise he could be released from the Tower and proclaimed King.

Richard decides to visit the King at once and stir up more hatred and fear against Clarence. If he fails to move the King, then a murderer for Clarence must be found the next day.

He gambles that Edward will die shortly of natural causes and leave "the world for him to bustle in," but not alone. He will marry Lady Anne, the widow of Edward, Prince of Wales, son of King Henry VI. He admits as his thoughts ramble that he killed Anne's husband and her father-in-law. Cold and callous about it, Richard decides the only way to compensate Anne is to marry her and "become her husband and her father." He would not do it for love, but for a close intent," which was likely the great wealth left her by her father.

As the scene ends he realizes his thoughts are racing ahead of him, and he determines that before anything else can be accomplished his two brothers, Edward IV and Clarence, must die.

SUMMARY

The opening scene is important for the quick but accurate impression it gives of Richard, Duke of Gloucester, later King Richard III, principal character in the play.

1. Richard's soliloquies and conversations show that he will not tolerate those who impede his ambition to be king. Without emotion he reveals that he has already committed two murders, namely King Henry VI and his son, Edward, Prince of Wales. His villainy can be blamed to an extent on his deformity, to which he refers in this scene and throughout the play. It has become an obsession with him.

2. The scene also shows the fitful side of Richard's character. As the play opens he declares he is not made to be a lover, but a few minutes later he plans woo and marry the wealthy young widow, Lady Anne.

3. The Duke of Clarence is no match for his brother's evil and hypocritical mind. Richard calls him "simple," yet a few years before he had aided his two brothers (Richard and the present King, Edward IV) in stabbing to death Edward, Prince of Wales, son of Henry the VI. (Compare *Henry VI*, Act V, sc. 5). Clarence appears as a pathetic figure, his life at the mercy of his brothers. In his short meeting with Richard it is clear that he is fearful of displeasing him and so says very little.

4. Lord Hastings, as a staunch Yorkist, urged the proclamation of Edward IV as King of England. (Compare *Henry VI*, Act IV, sc. 7). When they meet neither admits that he suspects the other of underhanded dealings. But Hastings does imply that his imprisonment in the Tower was due to Richard's suspicions that he, Hastings, was too friendly with the King. Later in the play (Act III, sc. 4) Richard, as Lord Protector, demands his head as a traitor.

ACT 1 SCENE 2

This long scene opens several days later on a London street. A funeral procession is moving slowly along: an open coffin containing the body of King Henry VI is carried on attendants' shoulders and two gentlemen with swords are guarding it. The body is being transferred from a tomb in St. Paul's Cathedral to Chertsey. The only mourner is Lady Anne, the widow of Edward, Prince of Wales, son of Henry VI.

Anne speaks to the bearers of the coffin, telling them to put it down, that she wishes to rest and lament the untimely death of the King. She denounces most bitterly the murderer of her father-in-law and her husband, and declares the same murderer killed both. She wishes curses on him and any children he may have. Though she never names the murderer, it is evident that she is referring to Richard, Duke of Gloucester, who she knows slew her husband.

After this long lament, she orders the men to take up the coffin. As the procession starts again the Duke of Gloucester enters from a side street, and at his command the bearers again put down the coffin. Immediately Anne upbraids the men for obeying him. She violently denounces Richard and accuses him of the murder. Professing his love for her, Richard asks her not to be too bitter toward him. But this only infuriates her more. She asks the bearers of the coffin to see how the King's wounds are bleeding!

Comment

It was an ancient belief that when the murderer approached the body of his victim the wounds would begin to bleed.

Anne's ravings continue, and she heaps abuse on Richard as a "lump of foul deformity," and begs God to revenge the King's death. Richard, patient in his declarations of love, gently chides her that she knows "no rules of charity." He begs her to let him make excuse for what he has done. Finally, he insists that it was her beauty that caused him to commit the murders. But Anne continues to revile him and even spits at him. He insists that he is going through "a living death."

Comment

Anne's older sister Isabella had married the Duke of Clarence, and after bearing him two children had died a natural death. It has been said that historically Richard knew Anne before her marriage to Prince Edward and was even then in love with her.

Even the story of his own father's death, when often repeated by her father, the famous Duke of Warwick, never brought tears to his eyes; but her beauty has made him blind with weeping and if she is so vengeful-he hands her his sword, and, kneeling, bares his breast that she may stab him. On his knees he admits he killed King Henry, and also that he "stabb'd young Edward," her husband. It was her "heavenly face" that made him do it.

Anne lets the sword fall and calls him a "dissembler." He takes it up and offers to stab himself if she will bid him do it. Anne's attitude toward him softens, but she fears he is not truthful. She tells him to put up his sword. Richard asks if she has then forgiven him. She answers that she will tell him later. He offers her a ring and she accepts, saying "to take is not to give," meaning she will not give her word to marry him.

Richard offers to see to the burial of the King and suggests she return to her house. He asks her to bid him farewell, but she tells him "Imagine I have said farewell already."

When Anne has gone Richard orders the coffin to be taken to White Friars and await his arrival.

Comment

After Lady Anne had disinterred the body of King Henry VI from the tomb in St. Paul's Cathedral, she was on her way to reinter his body in Chertsey, a small town twenty-five miles South of London. After her meeting with Richard he ordered the King's body to be taken to White Friars, the Carmelite Monastery in London. This enabled him to keep Anne close by and to continue his romance with her. Since the King's widow, Margaret of Anjou, was exiled in France, Anne, his daughter-in-law, was the closest living relative to attend to his burial.

Alone on the stage, in a long soliloquy Richard ponders his strange wooing of Anne. He boasts he will have her but immediately declares, "I'll not keep her long."

Comment

Later in the play (Act IV, sc. 1) when Anne is summoned to be crowned Queen of England, she has forebodings that Richard will "shortly be rid" of her.

Richard is amazed at his ability to overcome her extreme hatred for him in one short meeting. He questions whether she has forgotten her husband whom Richard very decently praises as a gentleman. He compares his own misshapen figure with the gallant and handsome Prince. Perhaps he has understated his own looks if Anne can find him " a marvelous proper man." Highly pleased with himself, he will begin at once to study fashions, employ "a score or two of tailors to make him costly garments. But his business at hand is to get the body of King Henry in a tomb. Then he will report to Anne. Meanwhile, he bids the sun keep shining until he can purchase a glass and see his shadow as he passes.

SUMMARY

> The scene serves to introduce Lady Anne, an important character in the play, as she will marry Richard. She is just another victim of his cruel, degenerate mind. His sudden meeting with her was planned as the best way to present his case and at the same time to divulge the murders of her husband and father-in-law. This spontaneous and straightforward manner of attacking a problem is characteristic of Richard. He neither deliberates over what to do nor weighs results once a deed is done. What he does must fit his plans at the moment.

ACT 1, SCENE 3

The scene opens in a reception room in Whitehall Palace. It serves to bring Richard face to face with two avenging members of the royal family: Queen Elizabeth, wife of Edward IV, and Queen Margaret, the bitter-tongued widow of Henry VI.

Queen Elizabeth, Lord Rivers, her brother, and the Queen's son by a former marriage, Lord Grey, and discussing King

Edward's illness. The Queen fears for her own safety and that of the young princes, sons by her marriage to Edward IV, if he dies. As they talk, the Duke of Buckingham and Lord Stanley enter. They report that the King's health seems improved. Moreover, he has sent for his brother, Richard, Duke of Gloucester, and the Queen's brothers, to try to bring peace to the royal household.

Richard, Duke of Gloucester, enters with Lord Hastings and the Marquis Dorset, brother of Lord Grey. He is angry that the King has sent for him because people have been complaining that he is too stern. The Queen openly accuses Richard of disliking her and her children and of being envious of her advancement at court.

Comment

Obviously Richard is jealous of the Queen's seeming power over his brother, Edward IV. Richard later in the play (Act III, sc. 5) asserts that her marriage to Edward was irregular. Her first husband, Sir John Grey, a Lancastrian, was killed in battle. His lands and possessions were taken away by the Yorkists, Edward IV and his brothers. In self-defense Elizabeth made a personal plea to the King to restore her possessions because of her two sons. According to the chronicles, the King met her at the country manor house of her brother, Lord Rivers, and granted her request to return her wealth. Shortly after, he fell in love with her - she was "neither too wanton nor too bashful" - and without consulting his brothers or advisers Edward IV quickly married her. Report spread abroad that the marriage was irregular and the two children born of the marriage illegitimate.

In turn, Richard accuses the Queen of imprisoning the Duke of Clarence, which she swears is not true. Lord Rivers denies that she caused Lord Hasting's term in the Tower. The Queen is distraught at Richard's "bitter scoffs" and she threatens to tell the King how he has treated her. As she mourns over the "small joy" that she has had "in being England's Queen," Margaret, the widowed Queen of Henry VI, enters back stage. She comes slowly forward making asides on the sharp dispute between Richard and the Queen. (Asides are comments intended to be heard only by the audience.)

In the first of these asides she declares that the Queen should not be on the throne since Edward IV has usurped the Crown. Margaret claims that it belongs to her. She is deeply stirred when she hears Richard tell the Queen that she can report what she pleases about him to the King and that he is not afraid of being sent to the Tower. To Margaret Richard is a "devil" who killed her husband and her son. Unaware of her presence on stage, Richard continues to antagonize the Queen, inferring how as a nobody she had made subtle use of her widowhood to get on the English throne. He claims his one difficulty in dealing with the tangled affairs at Edward's Court is that he is too soft-hearted. He is "too childish-foolish for this world."

When Lord Rivers remarks that if Richard might one day be "our lawful King" the realm would be loyal, Richard denies any such ambition and declares that he "had rather be a pedlar."

Impatient with their glib remarks over the lawful occupant of the throne, Margaret advances and demands they listen to her. She angrily claims to be their lawful Queen. Richard denounces her and reminds her how his father, Richard, Duke of York, cursed her when she killed his son (Richard's brother) Edmund, Duke of Rutland, on the battlefield.

Comment

Compare part 3 of *Henry VI*. Act I., sc. 4. In a battle on the plains near Sandal Castle, Margaret, then Queen of Henry VI, took an active part in directing the fighting. After the young Duke of Rutland was slain, his father Richard, Duke of York, was taken prisoner. She mockingly put a paper crown on his head and then, with the Lancastrian Duke of Clifford, stabbed him to death.

Cassandra-like, Margaret dominates the scene, heaping curses on Richard and taunting those who call her a "lunatic." Before she leaves she warns Buckingham, for whom she professes some friendliness, to beware of Richard. "Sin, death, and hell have set their marks on him;/ And all their ministers attend on him."

When Margaret goes, Richard, contrary to the others, pities her and repents the wrongs that he did to her. The Queen denies having ever wronged her, though Richard jibes that as Queen she is enjoying the wrongs done to Margaret. His mistreatment of her as well as that of his brother Clarence was to aid their brother Edward to gain the throne. He sneers that Clarence is nicely "frank'd up" (imprisoned) for his pains. Lord Rivers gives a caustic reply, taunting Richard for his "Christian-like conclusion."

Sir William Catesby, a gentleman of the King's household, enters with word that the Queen and the nobles have been summoned by the King.

Left alone, Richard takes deep satisfaction in his "secret mischiefs" that include the imprisonment of Clarence and placing the blame on the Queen. He comments how neatly he has clothed his "naked villany." He has done it "With old odds and ends stol'n out of Holy Writ/ And seems a saint, when most I play the devil."

He pauses to greet the two hirelings whom he has engaged to kill Clarence. They agree to "dispatch this thing" and ask him for the warrant. Richard gives the warrant he had gotten from Edward IV for the death of Clarence. But the order which the King had subsequently sent to the Tower counterdemanding the warrant Richard has intercepted and kept.

Among the instructions that Richard gives them is a warning to act quickly and not listen to the pleas of Clarence: he speaks well and may provoke their pity. When they have their work they are to go to his palace, Crosby Place, for their fee.

SUMMARY

This long scene is vital to the play in that it presents the underlying **theme**. It confirms the diabolical side of Richard's character:

1. The serious illness of the King brings to the surface the underlying discontent in the royal household. This underscores the play's **theme**, namely, quarrelling among the heads of government leads to its overthrow and paves the way for a despot to seize control.

2. The possibility of the King's death poses the question: What will become of the Queen and her children should Richard be made Royal Protector? The Queen expresses her deep anxiety over the problem. Here Shakespeare foreshadows the tragic fate of the young princes in the Tower.

3. To shift any suspicion from himself for imprisoning Clarence, Richard places the blame on the Queen. She vigorously denies it, but he intends to pursue it as it will continue to pave his way to the throne in liquidating members of her family.

4. Margaret's cursing of Richard and her dire prophecies bring an eeriness to the mood of the play. She is a kind of avenging Fury. Mentally unbalanced from the tragedies she has undergone-murder, exile, and false accusations-she excites pity. Even Richard remarks after she leaves that he feels sorry for her. His spontaneous reaction to Margaret is not unlike his violent assertions of love after the scornful abuse heaped on him by Lady Anne.

5. Richard's pity is only a fleeting thing and his satanic wit returns. He delights in the nimble way he can play the saint or the sinner with no display of conscience. His last word to Clarence's murderers is "Go, go, dispatch." The audience feels no suspense. He has cast a hypnotic spell over Evil, and it is fascinating to watch it do his bidding.

ACT 1: SCENE 4

This scene, which takes place the same evening, is laid in a room in the London Tower. Brackenbury, the Keeper of the Tower, listens patiently to the Duke of Clarence relate the ghastly dream he has had. He dreamed he had escaped from the Tower and with his brother Richard was on a ship bound for France. At the suggestion of Richard they walk on deck. Clarence tells that his brother "stumbled" and knocked him overboard.

While he floundered in the sea he wished to die, though the thought of dying terrified him. As he sank into the waves he imagined he saw the old wrecks of ships, fish gnawing on the bodies of the crew, great jewels, "heaps of pearls" and gold "scatter'd in the bottom of the sea." Brackenbury twits him on having time to think of riches when he was so close to death.

Clarence relates that when the waves finally engulfed him he did not wake but thought that he crossed the River Styx and came to the lower world, the "kingdom of perpetual night." There he saw the souls of those he had wronged: his father-in-law, Richard, Duke of York, who accused him of treason: and Prince Edward, heir of Henry VI, who cried to the Furies to avenge his murder by Clarence. A legion of fiends tormented him with their howling.

After relating the dream Clarence admits to Brackenbury that he had committed wrong deeds, but that he had done them for the King, his brother, Edward IV. He is grieved that his brother has been so cruel as to imprison him. But Clarence prays to God to avenge him alone for his crimes, and he asks Him to spare his wife and children.

Comment

Historically, Lady Isabella, the wife of Clarence, had died some months before he was confined in the Tower.

Wearied from recounting his frightening dream, Clarence falls asleep. As Brackenbury muses on the dangers and trials that beset royalty, two murderers enter with a warrant, signed by the King, to deliver Clarence to them. He gives them the keys, points to the sleeping Clarence and retires to tell the King he has discharged his duty.

The First and Second Murderers, as Shakespeare refers to them, discuss the murder they are about to commit. The Second Murderer has a "kind of remorse." His companion accuses him of being a coward and reminds him of the reward Richard has promised them. The Second Murderer blames his hesitancy on conscience, and he rattles off all the times in a man's life when it makes "a coward" of him; "A man cannot steal, but it accuseth him"; and "if a man swears, it checks him." And so on.

Fighting off the pricks of conscience, they discuss how they will murder Clarence. They decide to knock him unconscious, then stab him and throw him into an outer room where he will be taken for a drunk. The Second Murderer suggests killing Clarence while he sleeps, but the First Murderer objects. He thinks they should reason with him.

Clarence is finally awakened by their talk and demands to know who they are. He suspects their intent is to murder him, and they admit they are to kill him by the King's order. Making a desperate plea for his life Clarence insists he has committed no wrong; he has had no trial at court and the deed will bring eternal damnation on those who commit it.

The Murderers accuse him of Prince Edward's death. Clarence insists that was done for love of his brother, Edward IV. While they banter with him, the murderers reveal to Clarence that his brother Richard has sent them there "to destroy" him. Clarence insists it cannot be true, and recalls how Richard promised to have him freed from the Tower.

When the Murderers bid him make his peace with God, Clarence asks, "A begging prince what beggar pities not?" The First Murderer answers "Ay," and stabs him. He carries the body off stage. The Second Murderer is remorseful over the "bloody deed," and like Pilate would wash his hands "of this most grievous murder." He tells the First Murderer to keep the fee and he repents that Clarence is slain. The First Murderer calls him a coward. He declares that as soon as he collects his "meed" he must get away from London.

SUMMARY

In this grim scene Shakespeare presents a powerful interplay of conscience and guilt complex. Five persons are involved in the scene: Richard, though he never appears; Brackenbury, Keeper of the Tower; the two hireling murderers; and Clarence, the victim, brother of Richard and King Edward IV.

Richard, as instigator of the crime, bears the greatest moral guilt:

1. He plans the murder;

2. He intercepts the King's warrant countermanding Clarence's death; he gives the murderers the original warrant;

3. He hires the two murderers.

From the moment he planned his brother's murder (Act I, sc. 1), Richard has no qualms of conscience: if he is to gain the throne Clarence must be gotten out of the way. It is his first murder in the play and is convincing evidence of the immoral deeds to which he will stoop to gain his ends. From Richard's first appearance in the play he has courted evil, no matter how vicious, as a way to attain his ends. It is important to note that as a hero he shows no growth of character, one of the weaknesses of the play.

Brackenbury, Keeper of the Tower, is guilty in that he suspects the forgery but accepts the warrant and acquiesces to the murder. He attempts to relieve his conscience by saying "I will not reason what is meant hereby." So doing, he will be "guiltless of the meaning."

The sardonic humor of the two Murderers who jest over the stumbling blocks that conscience erects for them shows Shakespeare's art in handling situations involving serious moral issues, and in language that is virile, colorful, and direct. To the First Murderer the killing of Clarence is just a well paid job. To the Second Murderer the task becomes a brutal thing, and he loses courage. He remembers God's commandment against murder, but when his friend reminds him of the fee they have been promised his "holy humor" apparently changes. But his willingness is only a pose, and both conscience and natural fear finally deter him. Pretending to scoff at conscience he satirizes the ways this "blushing shame-faced spirit that mutinies in a man's bosom" can affect him. He notes that "conscience is always "turn'd out of towns and cities" 'as it is a "dangerous thing." Then, managing to take no part in the murder and accepting no fee, he believes that he is free of any guilt. As an accomplice he is morally guilty, though to a lesser degree than his companion who commits the murder.

Clarence is not an innocent victim. He has admitted murder and tries to assuage his guilt by claiming he did it to aid his brother. Emotion warps his reason, and in a desperate plea for his life, he insists: "If God will be avenged, He doth it publicly." If they murder him in secret, the murderers will then take "the quarrel from His powerful arm."

In setting forth the philosophy of guilt in this act, Shakespeare pursues the same reasoning that motivates all of his great tragic dramas, namely, "The wages of sin is death."

RICHARD III

TEXTUAL ANALYSIS

ACT II

ACT II: SCENE 1

In a room in the Palace of King Edward IV a colorful gathering of the nobles at his Court is awaiting him. Among those present are the Queen, her sons, Dorset and Grey, Rivers, Hastings and Buckingham. Showing signs of his grave illness, Edward enters, leaning on the arm of an attendant.

The King happily greets those present, mentioning his "good day's work" in bringing a semblance of union among the factions in his kingdom. He feels his death is imminent and wishes to depart leaving his friends in peace. He insists that Lord Hastings, a firm Yorkist, embrace Earl Rivers, brother of the Queen and, like her, unfriendly to him. Each swears "perfect love" for the other. (See *Henry VI*, part 3, Act IV, sc. 6).

Feeling that the display of affection he is witnessing could be insincere, he asks the Queen to let Lord Hastings kiss her hand and do it without pretense. The Queen promises to forget their former hatred, and to seal it the King calls on the Marquis of Dorset, son of the Queen by her first marriage, to embrace Hastings. Then the Duke of Buckingham, friend of Richard, swears fealty to the Queen and her allies.

As the King is voicing regret over the absence of Richard, he enters and wishes the King and Queen "a happy time of day." He is pleased to hear that the King has made "peace of enmity, fair love of hate" among those gathered about him.

Immediately, Richard claims he loves peace. To those present he feigns true friendship, asking forgiveness if he committed a wrong, and declares it is "death to me to be at enmity." He closes a long speech thanking God for his "humility."

The Queen takes him at his word and would celebrate this peaceful union with a holiday. She quickly remembers the King has not mentioned his brother Clarence. All present are aghast when Richard tells that Clarence is dead. He pretends to think they knew it. The King insists that his order was reversed but Richard lies to him, saying that a cripple bore the "countermand" and it arrived too late.

Emotionally overcome by the tragic news of his brother's death, which instantly blights his bright hopes for peace, King Edward has scarcely time to answer Richard when Lord Stanley, Steward of the King's household, hurries on stage. He begs a "forfeit" (an acquittal) from a charge of homicide against his servant. The request disturbs the King-he can help a servant, but is now unable to help his brother. He feels stinging remorse for Clarence's death. He tries to shift the blame to those around him. Why, he asks, did they not come to him and remind him of all the kind things Clarence had done in helping him to the throne? They knew he was in prison, yet none "would once plead for his life." Edward goes off stage lamenting that he and each of them will feel God's justice.

As the scene ends Richard and the Duke of Buckingham are left alone on the stage. Richard pretends he is indignant at the rash murder of Clarence. He notes that the "guilty kindred of the Queen look'd pale" when they heard it. He is quite satisfied that "God will revenge it." Buckingham goes with him to offer "comfort" to Edward.

SUMMARY

This scene is a study in remorse of conscience and the sometimes foolish means it suggests to wipe away guilt.

1. The weakness and gullibility of Edward IV serve as a foil for the quick and subtle mind of Richard. He has been able to dupe Edward by the simplest kind of trickery-dreams and "drunken prophecies."

2. Except for the Queen none of Edward's Court has praise or real affection for him. He is a pathetic figure trying, too late, to create a united "league" among the nobles at his court.

3. Richard purposely delays his appearance. When he enters he forces attention on himself with a long speech fawning over peace, enjoying the last sarcastic jibe - thanking God for his "humility." The Queen catches Richard unawares when she asks for Clarence. The King is silent. Richard, suspicious of her meaning, states she has "flouted" him in the royal presence. This forces him to declare that Clarence is dead.

4. All are horror stricken. Edward insists that someone "reversed" the order. Nemesis has finally caught up with him and he must defend himself. He attempts Richard's unfailing tactics of shifting blame but lacks the mental stamina to make his charges convincing. If Clarence had done all the good for which Edward credits him, if each one present "has been beholden to him" for some kindness, why, in the first place, did Edward listen to charges of treason against him? Who made the charges? Why does he not mention Richard? The answer is partly fear. He was too enfeebled now to risk antagonizing Richard.

The character of Edward as a ruler is nicely put in Plato's comment, quoted by William Baldwin in his "Address to the Nobility and All Others in Office" in The Mirror For Magistrates; "Well is that realm governed in which the ambitious desire not to bear office."

Edward had helped murder Henry VI and his son and so put himself, a Yorkist, on the throne. He had said to the dying Warwick on the battlefield, "Edward will always bear himself as king;/ Though fortune's malice overthrow my state,/ My mind exceeds the compass of her wheel." (part 3, *Henry VI*, Act IV, sc. 3).

5. Richard realizes that Edward's Queen is a severe threat to his ambition to rule. He must destroy her family and her children. They will be his next victims. If she can be made to appear guilty of Clarence's murder, his battle is won. Hence his remark to Buckingham, "How that the guilty kindred of the Queen/ Look'd pale when they did hear of Clarence's death?"

Richard knows his remark to Buckingham will eventually find its way into Court gossip. This would at least confuse the events surrounding the death of Clarence. Nor would his brotherly love go unnoticed if the gossipers heard he went immediately "to comfort" the King.

6. This scene places Richard in the ranks of Marlowe's heroes, but he is more agile than Tamerlane or Faustus in leaping from one evil deed to the next, yet just as sure-footed.

ACT II: SCENE 2

This scene takes place several days later. In a room in the King's palace the Duchess of York, mother of King Edward and Richard, is talking with her young grandchildren, the son and daughter of Clarence. She tries to conceal from them that the actual cause of her tears is their father's death, not King Edward's illness.

Comment

The Duchess of York, widow of Richard, Duke of York, was Cicely, daughter of Ralph Neville, first Earl of Westmoreland. The Duke was killed at the battle of Wakefield in 1460. To excite pity for her Shakespeare has made her eighty years of age, though historically she was almost twenty years younger.

With the suspicion common to children they think something has happened to their father, or why does she keep saying: "O Clarence, my unhappy son!"

Comment

The pathos of this scene provides momentary relief from the treachery and intrigue that has so far dominated the action of the play.

When the Duchess says that their father is "lost" the son is quick to interpret her remark as meaning death, and he declares that King Edward is responsible for it. He knows God will revenge it and will pray daily that He does. Though the Duchess tries to shield the King's guilt the children disbelieve her. They have it on the word of their Uncle Richard that the King ordered it and "was provoked to't by the Queen." He says their Uncle Richard has been very gentle with them. He had wept as he kissed them and promised he would be a father to them. Saddened that Richard should stoop so low in his deceitful ways, the Duchess calls him at once "her son and her shame."

She is interrupted by the loud weeping of the Queen who enters with her brother, Rivers, and her son, Dorset. She reveals that the King has died. The Duchess is deeply moved and complains how death has now left her only "one false glass" for her comfort, and Richard is her shame.

The children of Clarence are harsh toward their aunt, the Queen. Steeped in Richard's lies to them, they feel that she showed no sorrow for their father's death. In turn, they have none for her.

Dorset and Rivers try to comfort the two women by urging them to accept God's will in the case of Edward's death-a natural one. They also remind the Queen to look to the care of her son, who must be sent for immediately and crowned.

As they are talking Richard enters with Buckingham, Stanley, Hastings, Ratcliff and others. Richard greets the Queen as "Sister," telling her to "have comfort," weeping will not cure her woe. Pretending he had not seen his mother, the Duchess, he kneels for her blessing. When she asks God "to put meekness in thy breast," he mockingly adds in an aside, "and make me die a good old man!"

Buckingham had been prompted by Richard to take the initiative in urging the coronation of Elizabeth's son, Edward, Prince of Wales.

Comment

The Prince is at Ludlow Castle in Wales in the custody of his Uncle, Earl Rivers, Buckingham suggests that only a few attendants accompany the Prince to London. A "multitude" attending him might cause a rupture in the late King's effort to establish peace in the realm. Rivers opposes this. Richard keeps clear of the argument by expressing a hope that the King made peace "with all of us."

Hastings and Stanley agree with Buckingham that the Prince should have a small train accompany him. The Duchess and the Queen are asked by Richard to help decide who shall fetch the Prince from Ludlow.

Alone with Richard on the stage, Buckingham declares that it is essential that both of them go to Ludlow if they are to begin the project "we late talk'd of/ To part the Queen's proud kindred from the Prince." Playing the sycophant, Richard agrees to all Buckingham proposes. He calls him "My oracle, my prophet! my dear cousin,/ I, as a child, will go by thy direction." They are off for Ludlow.

SUMMARY

The mood of this scene from beginning to end is one of pathos. It advances the plot in permitting Richard to plan and execute his ruthless villainy without opposition.

1. We see the pitiful plight of Clarence's orphaned children.

2. Sympathy is evoked for the Duchess of York, Richard's mother.

3. It announces the death of King Edward.

4. Plans are laid to bring the Crown Prince to London for his coronation. This marks Richard's first move in his scheme to murder the children, King Edward's direct heirs.

5. Richard plumbs the lowest depths of villainy. He brings tragedy into the lives of the young and the aged. His deceit has warped the minds of the young son and daughter of Clarence: they hear him call on God for revenge, and now they begin to do the same.

6. When Richard meets his aged mother, the Duchess of York, we see her openly grief-stricken over the shame he has brought on the family. His unexpected reverence for her is tinged with scorn.

7. Richard flatters Buckingham in permitting him the initiative in the return of the Crown Prince to London. It will shift some of the malicious gossip from Richard.

So far none of his plans has gone awry. He can afford for a moment to sit back and play "the child."

Buckingham enjoys his role of mentor. He has a plan - he will find occasion to imprison Rivers and the rest of the Queen's family. Richard is appreciative, but he has the last word in the scene and it is a command: "Towards Ludlow then, for we'll not stay behind."

ACT II: SCENE 3

This scene takes place some few days later. Two citizens on a London street pass the time of day and exchange the latest news - the King's death. The Second Citizen has a very gloomy outlook for the state of the nation. A Third Citizen joins them. He and the Second Citizen see only trouble ahead. The First Citizen has faith in Edward's young son: "By God's good grace," he will rule well. The Third Citizen is not convinced, and his fears rest on the Scriptural text, "Woe to that land that's govern'd by a child!" The Second Citizen admits a council under him might rule well. This was the case "when Henry the Sixth/ Was crowned in Paris but at nine months old." The Third Citizen remarks that the infant French King had "virtuous uncles to protect His Grace," but that this is not the case at present. Young Edward has uncles, but Richard is "full of danger" and his mother's sons and brothers are too proud.

Comment

In John Rastell's *The Pastime of People* (1529) there is a brief account of Henry VI. "Henry the Sixth of that name and son of Henry the Fifth, being of the age nine months was proclaimed King of England [1521] . . . And then [Humphrey] Duke of

Gloucester, the King's uncle, was made Protector of England, and [John] Duke of Bedford, the King's other uncle, was made Regent of France. Also, in the eighth year of King Henry, he was crowned at Westminster . . . Also in the tenth year [1431] he was crowned in Paris." Shakespeare has erred in the date of the coronation of Henry the VI.

The First Citizen's comrades are too pessimistic. The Third Citizen feels certain that times will be troublesome; one can sense it, as he does the change of seasons: "When the great leaves fall, then Winter is at hand." The Second Citizen agrees that everyone is apprehensive. But the Third Citizen warns that men always fear a change: they had best place it all in God's hands. With this final word they go their way to the Justices.

SUMMARY

The importance of this very short scene is in the comparison it makes between the attitudes toward Richard of the average citizens of London and that of the nobles at Court. In each case Richard is feared, and this fear begets forebodings regarding the future of the realm. The chance meeting of the Three Citizens reflects the worry that has become widespread. Their philosophizing gives no hint that an outright threat of revolt is brewing against the government. Shakespeare is showing the competence of the average citizen in appraising the handling of civic affairs, though he played an insignificant part in them.

ACT II: SCENE 4

This is another short, homey scene (comparable to Act II, sc. 2). It takes place in a room in the palace; the Queen, her younger son Richard, Duke of York, and the Duchess of York listen as the Archbishop of York tells the latest news of the arrival of the Duke's brother, Edward, Prince of Wales. He has travelled by way of Northampton and Stony Stratford and should be in London the next day. The Duchess is anxious to see him and wonders if he has grown. When the Queen says "no," that her "son of York/ Has almost overt'aen him in in his growth," the young Duke, a delightfully precocious youngster, declares he is not at all pleased to outgrow his brother. Quite innocent of its poignancy, he describes an incident at supper one night with his uncles Rivers and Richard, who were remarking on his quick growth. He was very impressed with the old saying that his uncle Richard quoted, "Small herbs have grace, great weeds do grow apace." And since then the young Duke had wanted to grow slowly. The Duchess is quick to apply the saying to her son, Richard, noting how slowly he grew, and yet she implies he is not gracious.

Comment

The young Duke is pleased at the attention he is getting, and the repartee he keeps up with his grandmother shows a maturity beyond his years.

The Queen reproves the Duke for telling that he heard his "uncle [Richard] grew so fast/ That he could gnaw a crust at two hours old," and it was two years before he could get a tooth.

A messenger enters to give the disturbing news that Richard and Buckingham have imprisoned in Pomfret Castle the Queen's brother, Lord Rivers, and her elder son, Lord Grey, and with them Sir Thomas Vaughan. Both the Queen and the Duchess fear massacre and "domestic broils" will be the outcome.

As suggested by the Archbishop, the Queen and her son are escorted by him to Westminster sanctuary to take refuge.

SUMMARY

This scene has two functions:

1. It presents the attractive young Duke who with his older brother is destined to become a victim of Richard's scheme to gain the throne. Like Clarence's children, he is impressed by all that Richard says but has no real liking for him. He is an appealing youngster and is unaware of the sympathy and affection which his manly ways excite. The scene prepares for the quick and clever banter he carries out with his uncle, Richard, in Act III, sc. 1.

2. During the first two acts of the play Richard has taken giant strides to accomplish his evil ends and with success. Now, sure of himself, he becomes more ruthless. His own family, through the deaths of Edward and Clarence, is out of the way. Only Edward's children and the Queen's family remain. They will go quickly, too, and the imprisonment and pending execution of Rivers and Grey is the first step.

RICHARD III

TEXTUAL ANALYSIS

ACT III

ACT III: SCENE 1

The scene is late in the day following the flight of the Queen and her son to Westminster of sanctuary.

We are on a London street watching the triumphal return of Edward, Prince of Wales, who is to be crowned King of England. Trumpets sound as the young their approaches, accompanied by his Uncle Richard, Buckingham, Cardinal Bouchier, Catesby, and others.

Buckingham is the first to welcome Edward to the city. Before he can reply, his uncle remarks that he seems "melancholy." The Prince bluntly replies that he wanted "more uncles here to welcome" him. Richard describes them as too "dangerous." They have "sugar'd words" but poisoned hearts. He turns quickly to proclaim the arrival of the Lord Mayor and his train.

After a short greeting the Prince complains that his mother and brother should have arrived to greet him and wonders that Hastings has brought no news of them. As he speaks, Hastings arrives with word that the Queen and her young son have taken refuge in Westminster sanctuary. He would have brought the Duke, but his mother forbade him. Buckingham, secretly anxious to separate both sons from their mother, thinks the Duke should be seized as he has no right of sanctuary. This starts a discussion with the Cardinal during which Richard offers no opinion. Buckingham convinces the Cardinal that as a child the Duke has neither the "dealings" to deserve the place nor the wit to claim it. Accompanied by Hastings, the Cardinal agrees to fetch the Duke.

While they wait his arrival, Richard convinces the Prince that the Tower is the fit place for his brother and him to await the coronation. The Prince objects to the Tower-all towers. He questions whether Julius Caesar really built the London Tower, as it is said. Buckingham assures him that Julius Caesar began it. In an aside, Richard remarks that "so wise so young, they say do ne'er live long." To satisfy the Prince's curiosity he had to repeat the jingle but he quickly changed it to "without characters, fame lives long." If the Prince lives to be a man, he intends to emulate Caesar. He will "win our ancient right in France again." Richard's only comments are in asides that foreshadow the tragedy closing in on the young Prince.

When the Cardinal and Hastings arrive with the young Duke, Richard has a more difficult time with him - "a parlous boy/ bold, quick, ingenious, forward, capable;/ He's all the mother's from the top to toe." - so Richard, later, describes him. He reminds his Uncle about fast growth of weeds, seeing how the Prince has grown. He asks for his Uncle's dagger and gets it with the promise of a "greater gift" - a sword, the young Duke guesses. When the Prince taunts him for his sharp bantering with his Uncle, who has called him "little lord," the Duke makes an unfortunate reference to his uncle's deformity: "Because that I am little, like an ape,/ He thinks that you should bear me on your shoulders."

Comment

The precocious young Duke in altering his brother's remark mocks the hump on Richard's back. And comparing himself to an ape, or monkey, is not farfetched. The little animals were popular household pets. Holbein's portrait of the More family shows one climbing up the folds of Dame Alice's gown.

In an aside Buckingham tells Hastings "to be so cunning and so young is wonderful." Richard sharply stops the banter and without any ado maneuvers the Princes into the Tower against the childish fears of the Duke that he would be haunted by his Uncle Clarence's "angry ghost." His Grandma, the Duchess, had told him he had been murdered there. With a "heavy heart" the Prince leads the way.

When the Princes are safely locked up, and Buckingham and Richard are alone except for the attendant, Catesby, the former reverses his compliments about the young Duke. He fumes that the "prating" youngster must have been coached by his "subtle mother / To taunt and scorn you thus opprobriously." Richard agrees it was "no doubt" his mother's influence, but he lists a string of good qualities which suggests that he admires the Duke more that his brother, the Crown Prince.

He leaves to Buckingham the task of instructing Catesby how to sound out the allegiance of Lord Hastings to Richard's cause. Catesby doubts Hasting's affection for the Prince can be alienated. If he proves obstinate, Catesby is not to push the matter. As Catesby departs, Richard sends a greeting to Hastings to let him know his ancient enemies, Grey and Rivers, will die the next day. Still twitting him about Mistress Shore, this news is so good he should give her one more "gentle kiss." Catesby leaves, promising to bring news to Crosby Palace before they retire for the night. Buckingham wonders what they will do if Hastings will not yield to their "complots." Richard's answer is direct, "chop off his head, man." And, when he is King, Richard promises Buckingham for his loyalty "The Earldom of Hereford and the movables" of his brother, the late King.

SUMMARY

This is one of the most moving scenes in the play, depicting as it does the arrival in London of the Crown Prince for his coronation. We see him carefully stowed away in the Tower unaware that he is waiting for his execution, while his uncle usurps the Crown.

1. The scene serves to highlight facets of the character of each of those who are now vital to the plot. Richard has displayed, perhaps, the most contemptible trait of all. Heretofore his plotting and murders have been against adults as guilty of crime as himself: now to satisfy his ambitions he is using children in his royal game of blood-letting.

2. The attractive young Princes at the absolute mercy of Richard are pathetic. The Crown Prince, suspicious of the end, bravely leads the way to the Tower.

3. The friendly ties between Richard and Buckingham have seemingly grown stronger and will continue as long as the Duke needs him. Now Buckingham often

directs plotting, as he does to discover Hastings' loyalty to Richard. Though he has Richard fail to keep his word, Buckingham never doubts he will be the Earl of Hereford. He appears now for what he is, namely, an ambitious and ruthless sycophant, gambling on the whims of a neurotic despot.

ACT III: SCENE 2

The scene takes place about four o'clock the following morning. The house of Lord Hastings is the setting. A messenger from Lord Stanley has arrived there ahead of Richard's messenger. His message is urgent, hinging on a dream that Richard "had rased off" Stanley's helmet. Also, Stanley had learned that there are to be two Councils which he thinks may force enmity between him and Hastings. One way to shun the danger he foresees is for both of them to race north on horseback.

Hastings makes light of Stanley's worries. They will be together at one of the Councils: Catesby, whom he trusts, at the other, so they will know what goes on at each. As for dreams, Hastings is amused that he would "trust the mockery of unquiet slumbers." He bids the messenger tell his master to rise and come to his house. They will both go to the Tower and Stanley can see that the "boar" will be gentle towards them.

Comment

As Duke of Gloucester, Richard used a White Boar on his banner. During his first year as King, 1483, he founded the College of Heraldry, the corporation of the King's Heralds and Pursuivants of Arms.

Catesby enters as the first messenger leaves. Hastings is in a buoyant mood: he does not suspect the loyalty of this assistant of the late King. Hastings doubts Catesby's word that Richard wants to be crowned King. He is pleased to learn of the imminent execution of his enemies, Rivers and Grey, at Pomfret castle. But he tells Catesby that he will lose his own head before he will give his "voice on Richard's side." He feels so secure that he prophesies that he will send others "packing," even some who are dear to Richard and Buckingham. Catesby mentions that Hastings is quite highly thought of by them, but in an side, it is his head on the Bridge they really want.

Comment

It was a common practice when people were beheaded to display their heads on poles on London Bridge.

As they are talking Stanley arrives. Hastings jests about his dream of the "boar." But Stanley, who has a keen judgment regarding Richard, does not trust him. Rivers and Grey, he reminds Hastings, "had no cause to mistrust." When Hastings glibly tells him they are to be beheaded that day Stanley's reply is stern and portentous. "They for their truth, might better wear their heads/ Than some that have accused them wear their hats."

Comment

Richard, who met Hastings just after his release from the Tower (Act I, scs. 1 and 3), told him it was the Queen and her relatives who had caused his imprisonment. The Queen shortly after, when Hastings was present, bitterly denied the "vile suspects" he placed on her.

It nettles Hastings when he realizes that the implication is a jibe at him. He bids Stanley go along toward the Tower, that he will follow.

Hastings pauses to talk with a State Messenger who is passing. The last time they met, Hastings recalls, he was on his way as a prisoner to the Tower by "the suggestion of the Queen's allies." He cautions the messenger not to tell that on "This day those enemies are put to death;/ And I'm in better state that e'er I was." For the messenger's good wishes he tosses him his purse, saying "There, drink that for me."

A priest passing by stops to greet Hastings. The latter remembers he is in debt for the Priest's ministrations to him in the Tower. On "the next Sabbath," Hastings will "content" him. As they talk, Buckingham arrives on his way to the Tower. He jests that while Hastings' friends at Pomfret need a priest, Hastings has no shriving work in hand. As both Hastings and Buckingham go along their way to the Tower, Hastings remarks that he will "stay dinner there." In an aside Buckingham sneers, "And supper too, although thou know'st it not."

SUMMARY

1. This scene gives some relief from the constantly growing tension. It affords a character sketch of Hastings, a type of the vengeful and gullible noble who failed to halt Richard's mad march to be King. He will be one more to feel Margaret's curse. (Act III, sc. 2.).

2. Stanley stands untouched by the revenge scheme. After this scene he has an increasingly prominent part in resolving the plot.

ACT III: SCENE 3

This scene takes place the same day (not historically) in front of Pomfret Castle. Ratcliff, a noble henchman of Richard, is overseeing the execution of Rivers, Grey and Vaughan. The three nobles are conducted by a guard. Each of the men is vengeful. Rivers proclaims he is dying "For truth, for duty, and for loyalty." Pomfret he calls a "bloody prison" - the place where Richard II was "hack'd to death." Grey repeats Margaret's curse on them "For standing by when Richard stabb'd her son." Rivers corrects the order of the names of those Margaret cursed; he places Richard next to themselves, then Buckingham and Hastings.

Comment

Due perhaps to the stress of the moment and his vengeful feelings against Buckingham, Rivers errs in stating Margaret openly cursed Buckingham. Margaret says he has not harmed the Lancastrians, so he will not be "within the compass" of her curse. (Act I, sc. 3).

Rivers pleads God to "hear her prayers" for the others. But he asks that his sister, the Queen, and her sons be saved. They are told to move on by Ratcliff, and with a last embrace they go off to their doom.

Shakespeare shows the confused idea of revenge that permitted one to acknowledge "Revenge is mine, saith the Lord," and "Forgive thy enemies," then proceed to wreak vengeance on an enemy. In this he follows Marlowe's Faustus who begs for Divine mercy in his last hour of life, but gives no evidence of repentance. Neither Rivers nor Grey forgives his enemies, but asks God to turn Margaret's curse on her.

ACT III: SCENE 4

The Tower is the setting for this scene. It completes the action of scene 2 in which Stanley, Hastings and Buckingham are on their way to the Tower.

The members of the Council of which Hastings spoke in scene 2 are sitting around the table.

Those present are Buckingham, Stanley, Hastings, John Morton, Bishop of Ely, Ratcliff, Lovel, and others.

Comment

Bishop John Morton was a staunch supporter of the Earl of Richmond, Henry VII, who made him Lord Chancellor in 1487. Because of his personal knowledge of the conduct of Richard III as Protector and King, it is thought that he wrote or contributed data for Sir Thomas More's "The History of Richard III."

Hastings, in an exuberant mood, opens the Council with a terse statement of its business, namely, to set a date for the coronation of young Edward. Everything is ready for the occasion, according to Stanley. All that is needed is to name the day, and the Bishop suggests the following day. They realize that Richard, now Protector, must be consulted and will have the final say when he arrives.

Who present knows Richard's mind in the matter? Buckingham contradicts the Bishop that he does. Rather it is Hastings who should "soonest" know the Protector's mind - they are closer friends. Pleased with Buckingham's false flattery, Hastings denies he has had any word with Richard regarding the coronation.

Richard enters apologizing for being "long a sleeper." He learns from Buckingham the prominent part Hastings is taking in the Council. In fact, he is ready to act in Richard's stead and "Had pronounced your part - I mean your voice, - for crowning of the King." Richard says that he knows Hastings loves him well. He turns to the Bishop and remarks that he would like some of the fine strawberries he saw in his garden. The Bishop gladly orders his servant to fetch some.

Comment

This incident is related in the *History of King Richard The Third* by Sir Thomas More. At the Council meeting Richard, according to More, turned to the Bishop of Ely saying, "My Lord, you have verie good strawberries at your garden in Holborne; I require you, let us have a mess of them." The Bishop, pleased by the request, sent a servant to bring them.

As the Bishop leaves the room, Richard draws Buckingham aside to give him Catesby's report on Hastings. He repeats that Hastings said he "will lose his head e're he give consent" to crown any one king but the son of Edward IV. At Buckingham's suggestion they leave the council room to talk it over. While they are gone, Stanley, still suspicious of Richard despite his affable manner, thinks the coronation should be postponed for a time.

Just then the Bishop returns and asks for Richard. He is anxious to tell him that he has sent for the strawberries. Hastings gaily remarks how happy the Protector looks-he must have some plan that pleases him. He thinks Richard's face always betrays his heart. Stanley asks Hastings, "What of his heart perceive you in his face," today? Hastings, never suspecting that Catesby had betrayed his opinions concerning the Crown Prince to Richard, answers that the Protector's looks show that "with no man here he's offended."

Hastings barely finishes when Richard, in an angry mood, returns with Buckingham. He has discovered there are "devilish plots" and "damned witch craft" working against him. (See Hastings' remarks to Catesby in Act III sc. 2.) Richard asks what should be done with the perpetrators of them. In a display of loyalty, Hastings declares "they have deserved death." Richard bares his withered arm, which, he says, was caused by witchcraft - the consorting of Edward's wife, the Queen, that "monstrous witch," with the "harlot strumpet Shore."

Comment

Charges of witchcraft against both men and women were frequent during the War of the Roses. It was an expedient way to prosecute political enemies. Death by burning was one penalty imposed by the secular courts at the time.

Hastings fumbles again, saying "If they have done this thing, my gracious lord - " Brusquely interrupting, Richard points to him as the traitor, declaring "Off with his head! Now, by St. Paul, I swear/ I will not dine until I see the same." Telling his henchmen Ratcliff and Lovell to "look that it be done," Richard asks the others who "love" him to follow.

Left alone, Hastings realizes his mistakes. He blames himself for not heeding Stanley's warnings. He was too vengeful on hearing of the beheadings of Rivers and Grey, and now Margaret's curse has fallen on him. As he is led off stage he pities England, and prophesies dire times for the nation under "bloody Richard."

SUMMARY

This scene shows the despotic rule that Richard established as Protector.

1. The fear that the Queen's prestige may curb his power haunts Richard. But he cannot get rid of her as easily as the ambitious and willful nobles. It is possible, however, to discredit her as a witch and with Mistress Shore, a friend of Hastings, make her in part responsible for his deformity.

2. On the pretext that Hastings, the Lord Chamberlain, a partisan of the Queen, is plotting to destroy him, Richard can execute him for treason. Such an offense will quell any public sentiment for him.

3. The scene provides an interesting contrast between Rivers and Hastings, particularly in the remarks each makes as he goes to the block: Hastings has a deeper sense of moral values than does Rivers (Act III, tc. 2). While Rivers goes off praying curses on his enemies, Hastings recognizes the small value of the "momentary grace of mortal men,/ Which we more hunt for than the grace of God!" Then Hastings likens those who trust in men's promises to the drunken sailor on a mast who sways back and forth and is ever in danger of tumbling into the deep.

ACT III: SCENE 5

This scene takes place the same day, outside the Tower and a short time after the execution of Hastings.

As the scene opens, Richard and Buckingham are seen on the Tower walls wearing rusty armor and looking harassed and bedraggled. They are staging a mock duel with an imaginary foe who is avenging Hastings' death. Richard coaches Buckingham how to be "mad with terror." But Buckingham declares he "can counterfeit the deep tragedian" and is as adept at "ghastly looks" as he is with "enforced smiles."

Catesby has been sent to bring the Lord Mayor and his train. When he arrives, a crowd has gathered outside the Tower. Richard and Buckingham are racing back and forth shouting commands as if they are warding off blows from an attacker. Buckingham starts to tell the Lord Mayor why they have sent for him, but Richard interrupts with a plea to be careful, there are enemies nearby.

Lovell enters with Hastings' head, holding it up so all can see "that ignoble traitor." Richard, pretending he is overcome by grief, weeps as he eulogizes Hastings as "the plainest harmless creature/ That breathed upon the earth a Christian." Richard tells how he loved him as a confidant until he found that Hastings was consorting with Mistress Shore and covering his vice with a "show of virtue."

Buckingham sees him only as a "subtle traitor." He accuses Hastings of plotting this day in the council house to "murder me and my good Lord of Gloucester."

Richard assures the Mayor except for "the extreme peril of the case,/ The peace of England and our person's safety," they would never have proceeded so rashly. The Mayor praises them. It will be a warning to others. But he was not surprised at Hastings after he had taken up with Mistress Shore.

The death sentence was carried out with greater haste than they intended, Buckingham declares. They wished that the Mayor might have heard him confess the purpose of his treason. Then the Mayor could have informed the citizens, and they would not have blamed them and would not "wail his death."

The Mayor is satisfied with the justice of the case. Having so neatly hoodwinked the Mayor, they politely bid him farewell.

He is scarcely out of hearing when Richard reveals Buckingham's next task. He must overtake the Mayor on the way to the Guild Hall and get across to him,

(a) That Edward's children are likely bastards.

Comment

Edward had put a citizen to death for saying that the King "would make" his son heir to the crown. This citizen has been identified as a well-to-do tradesman named Walker. The execution of this man appears in a list of misdeeds committed by Edward IV and presented to Richard before his coronation. It was later turned into an Act of Parliament. Edward's crimes are greatly exaggerated.

(b) That Edward had an insatiable and indiscriminate lust.

(c) That Edward himself was likely illegitimate: (his father was away at the wars and by computing the time found the child was not his, nor did he resemble Warwick, Richard's father).

(d) Buckingham must be guarded in pressing this last issue because Richard's mother, the Duchess, is still alive.

Buckingham assures Richard he will "play the orator." If he is successful, Richard will await him at Baynard's Castle "with reverend fathers and well-learned bishops."

Comment

This castle was built on the banks of the Thames by a Norman noble named Baynard. He is said to have erected it in the time of William I.

To be certain that at least two prominent clergy are on hand, Lovel is sent to fetch Dr. Shaw, the Mayor's brother: Catesby, to bring Friar Penker, Provincial of the Augustinian Friars. Meanwhile Richard, alone now, muses that he will give a "privy order" that will keep "the brats of Clarence out of sight." No one will be allowed to see them.

SUMMARY

This scene is necessary to further Richard's plan to seize the crown.

1. The humbug that Richard and Buckingham make in fighting an imaginary enemy is contrived to gather a crowd. It will provide a perfect setting for Richard to pass for a brave and loyal Protector. He gambles that neither the Mayor nor the gullible citizens will ever suspect him. He has shown the way to deal with enemies - "Off with their heads."

2. Of all the nobles surrounding Richard, Hastings has the least worldly wisdom. His arrogance has caused him to misjudge everyone - Edward, the Queen,

Buckingham and, finally, he fails to see Richard as a blood-thirsty throne-seeker and falls into his trap.

3. The moral precept of the scene, however, comes from Hastings in his realization of the futility of hunting for men's favors, rather than for God's.

4. Though Richard is aware of the citizens' power to crush him, yet, at the crucial moment, he must trust others to urge his cause with them.

5. Fortune has smiled on Richard after each of his bloody sallies. As he nears the top of her wheel, will she hurl him down? Richard, as he must, gambles that she won't. Buckingham and the Lord Mayor, he knows, are weak reeds to lean on, but he has found every man and woman weak if goaded on by flattery and golden promises. Buckingham has already been promised an earldom and is not likely to forget it. If Richard can dupe the citizens he has no fears that the ecclesiastics will spurn him - they have almost no choice - nor will the "brats of Edward." His plans are laid, and he has no fears that they will go awry.

ACT III: SCENE 6

This very short scene is on a London Street.

A scrivener muses over an indictment pertaining to the beheading of Lord Hastings. The original draft took eleven hours to draw up. The scrivener remarks that it also took him eleven hours to copy it. He will post it in St. Paul's.

Comment

The portico of the old St. Paul's Cathedral was used as a place to post legal and personal notices.

The scrivener is not satisfied with the accusations against Hastings. He notes that Hastings was "untainted, unexamined, free, at liberty," within five hours of his death. No one is so "gross" as to not mistake it for a device, yet no one is so bold to say so. It is a bad world, he thinks, when "such ill dealing" is concealed.

SUMMARY

The scene establishes the following points:

1. Richard fearing serious consequences has Hastings' execution made legal.

2. The average citizen, however, can see through the sham. Hastings, at the time of his death, had not been dishonored nor subject to legal questioning; he was at liberty before he was seized and executed.

3. The London citizen has begun to deplore the condition of the country when the people's free speech and personal rights are violated.

4. It is the first inkling of Richard's unpopularity and might easily be fanned into an uncontrollable flame.

ACT III: SCENE 7

This scene follows a few hours after Scene 5 in Baynard Castle.

Richard and Buckingham are alone in the courtyard. When Richard learns that "The citizens are mum, say not a word," regarding the Crown, he demands if Buckingham mentioned the illegitimacy of Edward's children. Buckingham declares he did, and gives him a point by point resume of his harangue to the crowd. He made much of Edward's supposed engagement to Elizabeth Lucy, of his unbridled lewdness in London, and of his bastardy.

Comment

Edward IV had had an affair with Elizabeth Lucy prior to his marriage with Lady Elizabeth Grey. To obstruct this marriage his mother, the Duchess of York, declared he was affianced to Elizabeth Lucy, who denied it. There were other grounds for Richard's illegitimacy claims, as Edward had been married to Lady Eleanor Butler, widow of Lord Butler of Sudley. In the Parliament which Richard convened he used these grounds to have Edward's children made illegitimate.

As a boost to Richard's pride Buckingham had also added that Edward did not resemble their father, Richard, Duke of York, as Richard did. The latter was the image of his father, both in "form and nobleness of mind." Buckingham told also how victorious Richard had been in the Scottish wars, and the wisdom he had in peace. When he had shown Richard as bounteous and full of virtue and "fair humility," he called on those that did love their country's good to cry "God save Richard, England's royal King!"

Richard asks if the citizens responded. Buckingham replied, "They spake not a word." They stared and looked deadly pale, he said. He upbraided them. The Mayor explained that the crowd was unaccustomed to being spoken to directly: a recorder always relayed the Court's message. But the recorder was no more successful. A few of Buckingham's hirelings threw their caps in the air and about ten cried, "God save King Richard!" Then, Buckingham said, he took "vantage of those few" and thanked the citizens for their applause. It proved, he said, their wisdom and love for Richard.

It is hard for Richard to believe that these "tongueless blocks" would not speak. Anxiously, he asks if the Mayor and his train will meet him. Buckingham had at least interested the Mayor who is on his way now to the Castle.

Buckingham ventures some suggestions how Richard should receive him: he should pretend some fear; be difficult to gain access to; it would look well for him to be reading a prayer book and stand between two churchmen; and not be easily won over. Richard must "Play the maid's part; still answer nay, and take it."

Before he can say more, the Mayor knocks, and Richard hurries out of sight. Buckingham welcomes the Mayor and advises him that it is difficult to get an audience with the Duke. Catesby brings word that Richard asks Buckingham to come to see him the following day. He is in meditation with two right reverend fathers and no worldly business can interrupt him. Catesby is sent back to urge a meeting with the Mayor and Alderman. There are "matters of great moment" that touch the general good to be discussed.

While Catesby is about his errand, Buckingham uses the interim to compare Richard's holiness with the vices of his late brother, the King, though the latter is not named. But Buckingham feigns great fear that Richard will not accept the "sovereignty of the nation." The Mayor prays God that he will.

Catesby brings word that Richard is worried that Buckingham has "assembled" so many citizens. The latter sends back word that he, as well as all present, "come to him in perfect love," Buckingham moralizes how devout men, like Richard, are loathe to leave their "zealous contemplation."

In a gallery just above them, the Mayor spies Richard with the two clergymen. Buckingham is quick to point to the prayer book in his hand-a true sign of a holy man. He addresses Richard as "Famous Plantagenet" and regrets interrupting his devotions. Richard begs him not apologize but tell him the purpose of the visit. He is afraid he has done "some offense." Buckingham assures him he has in not becoming King. In a long speech Buckingham musters all the reasons why he should accept. Richard's answer is a cleverly devised rejection, coming finally to the point that Edward has left "royal fruit" in the young Crown Prince, "The right and fortune of his happy stars;/ Which God defend that I should wring from him!"

Buckingham praises Richard's nicety of conscience. Later, in his long speech, he implies that the father, Edward IV, of this young prince is illegitimate.

Comment

In scene 5 of this act, Richard suggested his brother's illegitimacy, but Buckingham was to touch this lightly. Richard remarks, "You know my mother lives."

The House of York, he claims, is in great danger unless Richard accepts the crown. Richard cannot see why he should take on such a burden. Buckingham declares the young Prince will never reign. He pretends to be out of patience with Richard and starts to leave with the Mayor and the citizens.

At Catesby's urging Richard calls them back. Since they "buckle fortune" on his back, he will accept the Crown. Buckingham is the first to salute him, "Long live King Richard, England's worthy King!" Then all answer "Amen."

Buckingham asks when he wishes the coronation. It is settled for the following day. With the clergymen, Richard leads the way "to our holy work again."

SUMMARY

This scene brings Richard only a few steps away from his aim, namely, to ascend the English throne.

(1) It forces Richard to confront the citizens who are now aware of the move to proclaim him King.

(2) With Buckingham's report of lack of response to his harangue, Richard, unprepared for this reaction, realizes he cannot force them to accept him. For the moment he is stunned.

(3) He must follow Buckingham's strategy and play hard to get. As a deceiver, Richard is perfect in the role:

(a) He pretends fear of the crowd.

(b) He stands in the gallery away from them and "protected" by two clergymen.

(c) He is unmoved by Buckingham's ardent plea to save his noble house from corruption" and to keep a true line of descent.

(4) It is typical of Richard that while he pretends to refuse the Crown he does not retire from the scene. To keep his villainy at its low level, Shakespeare allows the stooge, Catesby, to request Richard to recall the crowd. He does and accepts the Crown.

(5) Richard's acceptance speech is a piece of artful villainy that places all the blame on the crowd if "black scandal" reproach him.

RICHARD III

TEXTUAL ANALYSIS

ACT IV

ACT IV: SCENE 1

This scene takes place in front of the Tower, shortly after Richard has been crowned King.

Queen Elizabeth, her elder son Dorset, and the Duchess of York come forward to greet Lady Anne, accompanied by Lady Margaret Plantagenet, the young daughter of the murdered Clarence. The latter are on their way "to gratulate the gentle Princes" in the Tower.

Comment

Historically, Lady Anne married Richard about 1472, a year after her meeting with him while on her way to bury King Henry VI.

As they talk Brackenbury, the Keeper of the Tower, enters, and the Queen inquires about the health of the Princes. He assures her that they are well, but gives the disturbing news that the King has forbidden anyone to see them.

The Queen, and those with her, are unaware of the events of the previous day. They are amazed at the word "King." "Who's that?" she asks. Brackenbury corrects himself-he means, the "Lord Protector." Despite the ardent pleas of the three women Brakenbury declares he is bound by oath to refuse anyone admittance to the Princes.

As he finishes, Lord Stanley enters to summon Lady Anne to Westminster to be "crowned Richard's royal Queen." It is disturbing news. When Dorset tells his mother to be of good cheer, she pleads with him to flee to France and join Lord Stanley's step-son, Richmond. She fears for his life remembering Margaret's curse that she will die "Nor mother, wife, nor England's counted Queen."

Comment

Richmond is a step-son of Lord Stanley. His mother was Margaret Beaufort, one of the most learned and charitable women of her day. His father was Edmund Tudor, Earl of Richmond. Young Richmond was descended from the Lancastrians. Owen Tudor, his grandfather, married Catherine of France, widow of Henry V and mother of Henry VI. He is raising an army in France and will return to England to defeat Richard.

Stanley agrees that Dorset should leave immediately for France and will give him letters to Richmond. He cuts short the lament of the Duchess of York for the "cockatrice" that she has "hatch'd to the world" in Richard. He bids Lady Anne make haste to the coronation; but she will not leave until she has declared her folly in marrying Richard. She recalls how she repulsed Richard's affection for her; she repeats the curse that she wished for him and whoever would be his wife, namely, that she be more "Miserable by the life of thee/ Than thou has made me by my dear lord's death!" Since her marriage to Richard, she has always felt her own curse, and now, she believes, he "will shortly be rid" of her.

The Queen and the Duchess bid Lady Anne farewell. The Queen asks her to wait a bit and look back with her to the Tower. She gives what amounts to a tender eulogy for her young sons. She addresses the Tower as "Rude ragged nurse, old sullen playfellow/ For tender princes, use my babies well!" She implies their fate in her remark, "So foolish sorrow bids your stones farewell."

SUMMARY

The scene serves to bring into focus several divergent aspects of the play:

(1) The royal family sees their fears fulfilled when they learn Richard is crowned.

(2) The adamant manner of the Keeper in refusing to allow the women to see the Princes engenders greater bitterness toward Richard. Each event in the scene directly, or indirectly, contributes to it.

(3) From the moment that Lord Stanley enters to call Lady Anne to her coronation as Richard's Queen he plays an increasingly prominent role in resolving the

King's tragic downfall. His counseling of Dorset to flee England and join Richmond will put Richard for the first time on the defensive (sc. 2). It places Lord Stanley, wealthy and powerful, as his secret enemy. Stanley's conservative manner makes him more difficult to cope with than the cocky and presumptive Hastings and Buckingham. Consequently, Stanley is the only person close to him whom Richard fears.

(4) Lady Anne is a pathetic figure going off to her coronation. Nemesis is finally catching up with her. Though she cursed any woman who would marry him, now as his wife she reveals how the curse has returned to her. Her sufferings come not only from her own curse. Her father, Warwick, deserted the Yorkists and joined the Lancasters, and the curse he brought on his family fell on her husband, as his father's heir, and then on her.

(5) As the **protagonist** for the Yorkist cause Richard, at the moment, has become the great Avenger. Nemesis, greedy for its victims, uses him, and pushes back into history, making both the Lancastrians and the Yorkists pay who share or inherit any taint of wrong.

ACT IV: SCENE 2

This scene is in a room of state in the palace. Richard enters, already crowned. With him are Buckingham, Catesby, a Page, and attendants.

He is delighted with the pomp and ceremony and asks Buckingham to help him ascend the throne. His first words as

King are in praise of Buckingham, "Thus high, by thy advice/ And thy assistance, is King Richard seated." Almost immediately he begins to test Buckingham's loyalty. He wants to know whether Buckingham "be current gold indeed."

Though all may call him King, Richard is troubled because "Young Edward lives." Buckingham's reply, "True, noble Prince," nettles Richard. He reprimands him for being so dull. Richard wants "the bastards dead," and he wants it done quickly. Further, he wants Buckingham's opinion on it. When the latter begs time to think it over, Richard is at once suspicious. Catesby, in an aside, observes "The King is angry; see, he gnaws his lip."

When Buckingham leaves the room, Richard remarks he has no time to waste on "iron-witted fools," and none are for him who look at him with "considerate eyes." He comes down from the throne musing, "High-reaching Buckingham grows circumspect." Then, without more ado, Richard plans the death of the Princes. Through his Page he learns of Tyrell who will kill for "gold."

While the Page goes to fetch Tyrell, Richard, alone on the stage except for Catesby, declares if Buckingham has grown weary keeping up with him and must stop for breath, "well, be it so." As he is speaking Stanley enters with news that Dorset has gone to France to help Richmond.

The news brings the play to a **climax**. Richard is keenly aware that Richmond will be hard to conquer. His mind races on to defend himself. To prepare the public for Lady Anne's death, Catesby must rumor it about that she is "very grievous sick." When Catesby is slow to go Richard is impatient. To safeguard the throne, he must marry his brother Edward's daughter, or else the "Kingdom stands on brittle glass." He must also marry off Clarence's daughter to a "mean-born gentleman." As to Clarence's son, "the boy is foolish, and not to be feared."

Comment

The son and daughter of Clarence mentioned here appear in Act II, sc. 2, with their grandmother, the Duchess of York. Richard's remark in that scene, referring to him as "foolish," is not fair to the boy. Historically, he is said to have been badly mistreated. He was put to death by Henry VII, in 1499. He was the last surviving male of the Plantagenets.

But the Princes must be disposed of first. He recognizes the end of it all is uncertain. In a kind of desperate nonchalance he acknowledges, "I am in/ So far in blood, that sin will pluck on sin." But he remarks none of it creates pity or tears in him.

When the Page reenters with Tyrell, Richard loses no time engaging him to dispatch "those bastard brats in the Tower." Tyrell, fortified with a token, agrees to the task. When it is done, Richard wants immediate report. He promises Tyrell his love and preferment.

Buckingham returns to the room as Tyrell leaves, and tells Richard he has been considering the "question," meaning the murder of the children. But Richard is deaf to his remarks. He is completely engrossed in the knowledge that Dorset has joined Richmond. He implies to Stanley that serious consequences can result since Richmond is his wife's son. Stanley makes no reply.

Buckingham again tries to get Richard's attention, reminding him of the kingly gifts he had promised - the earldom of Hereford and "the movables." Richard ignores him. Stanley listens to Richard recount the prophecy of Henry VI, that Richard would be King when he was yet a "little peevish boy." He wonders why Henry was not able to prophesy his own death by Richard's hand. Richard repeats the word "Richmond." He tells Stanley how during a visit to Exeter the Mayor showed him the castle and mispronounced it "Rouge-mont." It startled him because an Irish bard had long before told him he would die soon after he saw Richmond.

During Richard's musing Stanley never interrupts. Buckingham interrupts the King several times to ask about his promised earldom. Exasperated with him, Richard demands the time of day. He compares Buckingham to a jack, the iron figures of men on the outside of old clocks that struck the hours, because "thou keep'st the stroke/ Betwixt thy begging and my meditation." Richard declares he is "not in the giving vein today." Boldly, Buckingham asks for a definite "yes" or "no" about the earldom. Irritated by his persistence, Richard walks off stage with Lord Stanley, fretting, "Thou troublest me; I am not in the vein."

Left alone, Buckingham sees his folly in placing confidence in Richard's promises. To avoid the same fate as Hastings, he leaves immediately for his castle in Wales.

SUMMARY

This scene, one of the most famous in the play, is the climax.

(1) Richard has arrived at the summit. Can he maintain his place? Ill gotten goods are difficult to keep, and he knows this well. The first test of loyalty for those about him is given to Buckingham. Remembering an oath of fealty to Edward's sons that he had sworn years before, Buckingham hesitates to agree to their murder (Act V, sc. 1). Richard wanted immediate

approval, not a well considered answer. When Buckingham failed to give it, he became a traitor in Richard's eyes.

(2) Lord Stanley is shrewd in his approach to Richard. He announces almost casually and without comment Dorset's defection to Richmond. He knows that Richard will leap into action and the less he says to him, the less danger there is of involving himself or his family. Throughout the scene he is careful to maintain this silence. Stanley is aware, despite Richard's offhand ramblings about the past, that he is being watched for even a change of expression that might betray his allegiance. To the end, Richard had respect for Stanley, but an instinctive mistrust for his word.

(3) Richard sinks to the lowest moral level in proposing to marry his niece. First, he must murder her two brothers. He forestalls any remorse of conscience for his foul schemes by despairing that he is so "far in blood," it is impossible to escape now. His acts from this point on are dictated by his will to keep the Crown regardless of the cost.

(4) The situation is full of tragic humor with Buckingham constantly interrupting Richard's musings with demands for the earldom promised him for his services. Richard ignores him.

ACT IV: SCENE 3

This scene, full of tragedy and pathos, takes place in a room in the King's palace.

Tyrell enters alone. In a long soliloquy he laments "this ruthless piece of butchery" - the murder of the young Princes. Though inured to crime, even the two assassins whom he hired, Dighton and Forrest, wept like children as they told him. He relives the scene, repeating the assassins' exact description of the murder. Dighton told that the boys were asleep with their arms around each other. A prayer book lay on the pillow. Forrest said that "almost changed my mind/ But O, the devil - " Dighton continued, "We smothered/ The most replenished sweet work of Nature,/ That from the prime creation e'er she framed." When they were dead, Tyrell went to look at them and has come to report the deed to the "bloody King."

When he hears the King's step, he goes to greet him as "my sovereign Lord!" Richard inquires if he will be happy over the news. Tyrell assures him he has done the "thing" he had been charged to do. Did he see them dead and buried? Tyrell did see them dead, but a priest buried them secretly. Richard dismisses him with the charge to return after supper and give him the details of the murders. Meantime, Tyrell was to think how Richard may do him "good."

Alone on the stage, Richard reviews what he has accomplished in blocking any challenge to his right to the Crown:

1 - He has imprisoned Clarence's young son. Clarence's daughter he has matche'd marriage to a nobleman." (Clarence's daughter married Sir Richard Pole. She became the mother of the great Reginald Cardinal Pole. During the Reformation she was beheaded by King Henry VIII.)

2 - Edward's sons "sleep in Abraham's bosom."

3 - Richard's wife, Lady Anne, has already "bid the world goodnight."

Comment

After Richard's remark there is no further mention of Lady Anne in the play, nor details concerning her death.

Now young Richmond wants to marry Edward's daughter Elizabeth to unite the Yorks and Lancasters on the throne. But Richard, "a jolly, thriving wooer," will go to her first.

His jubilant mood vanishes when Catesby hurries in with the news that John Morton, Bishop of Ely, has gone to the aid of Richmond; Buckingham, with a battalion of Welshmen, has also turned against Richard. Ely's defection disturbs Richard more than Buckingham's. But he concludes that discussing what tactics to pursue only causes delay. Catesby is ordered to "muster men;" Richard will prepare for battle at once.

SUMMARY

The turning point of the play which occurs in this scene is the first direct blow of retributive justice that jars Richard's sureness of his power to overcome fate. Shakespeare has timed it immediately after the repulsive murder of the children in the Tower. Tyrell's soliloquy quoting an actual description of the murders, as he heard it from the two assassins, does three things:

(a) It creates an impression of horror on the audience.

(b) It makes Richard so repugnant that only Shakespeare's art saves him from being classed as mentally diseased.

(c) It validates the slow heaping of vengeance on Richard until the end of the play.

As the scene closes Richard has come to realize he has no one to rely on but himself; "My counsel is my shield." He will fight for his right to the Crown. His indomitable will raises his hopes to such a pitch that he believes he can win against any odds.

ACT IV: SCENE 4

This very long scene takes place within a few days in front of the palace.

Queen Margaret is alone on the stage. She is as vengeful as in her first appearance (Act I, sc. 3). She sees prosperity on the wane among her enemies. Soon she will return to France, and she leaves with the hope that the future for them will be as "bitter, black, and tragical as it promises."

Comment

When Margaret appears in Act I, sc. 3, she prophesies doom for each of those who had wronged her family. Now she returns to see her words confirmed.

As Queen Elizabeth and the Duchess of York arrive, Margaret keeps out of their sight. The Queen sighs over the deaths of her "tender babes." In an aside, Margaret picks up her plea that the "gentle souls" of the children will hover about her. She would have them tell their mother that Divine Justice has now avenged them both-each has lost a son. When the Duchess mourns for her son, Edward IV, the scene becomes almost an antiphonal as the two mothers, and, later, Margaret, indulge their sorrows in bitter lamentations over their bereavements.

Elizabeth asks when did God ever "sleep while such a deed was done" In an aside Margaret answers: when her husband and son died. The Duchess, referring to the "world's shame" and to herself as a "living ghost," sits on the ground. Elizabeth sits beside her, wishing that the earth would as easily afford a grave as this "melancholy seat." She asks "Ah, who has any cause to mourn but I?" Coming forward, Margaret pleads, "If ancient sorrow be most reverend" that her sorrow be given "seniory." Addressing her remarks to the Queen, Margaret matches murder for murder in the two families.

Comment

Margaret feels Elizabeth usurped her own place on the throne and curses her for it.

The Duchess draws attention to her own sorrows. Like Margaret and Elizabeth she has lost a husband and a son by the assassin's knife. But her remark brings a heap of vicious invective on her for bringing Richard into the world, "That dog, that had teeth before his eyes." The old Duchess begs Margaret not to triumph in her woes; she has often wept for Margaret's. But her plea is unavailing and Margaret admits that she is "hungry for revenge." Now she is enjoying a surfeit of it. One by one those who wronged her have been mowed down by Richard. Now her only prayer is that she may live to say of him, "The dog is dead."

Elizabeth remembers Margaret's prophecy (Act I, sc. 3) that the day would come when she would wish her nearby to help her curse Richard. The remark launches Margaret's long speech-a veritable diatribe on Elizabeth for usurping her place as Queen. Half of the yoke that Margaret has long borne, Elizabeth now bears. But soon Margaret will leave it all to her.

Moved by her speech, Elizabeth asks her to wait and teach her how "to curse" her enemies. She must learn, Margaret counsels, to "Compare dead happiness with living woe." Then her own woes will sharpen her curses, and they will "pierce" as do Margaret's.

As Margaret leaves the Duchess impatiently asks, "Why should calamity be full of words?" They help nothing, Elizabeth replies, but "they ease the heart." If so, the Duchess urges Elizabeth to come with her, and with bitter words "smother /My damned son, that thy two sweet sons smother'd."

The Duchess warns that the drums announce Richard's approach, and tells Elizabeth they must "be copious in exclaims."

Richard and his train are starting off to war and asks who it is that "intercepts" him. The Duchess says it is she who might have "intercepted" him by strangling him in her "accursed womb." Both women ply him with questions where their loved ones are. Richard is irked by their railing on "The Lord's anointed." He orders a flourish of trumpets to drown their "exclamations."

A bitter dispute follows between Richard and his mother who detains him despite his refusal to listen to her. She quickly sketches his life from his birth to now-every moment of it has made earth a hell. If he so offends her, Richard asks to be let go his way. The Duchess pleads for a word more - "For I shall never speak to thee again." She places on him her "most heavy curse," which in the day of battle will tire him more than his "complete armour." Prophesying "bloody will be thy end," she leaves. Richard murmurs, "So."

Comment

In Gorboduc, by Sackville and Norton (1558), the first Elizabethan tragedy, Queen Videna, in cursing her son Porrex for the murder of his brother Ferrex, parallels the Duchess' curse on Richard. Videna asks "Can'st thou hope to 'scape my just revenge?" Again, she says, "The gods on thee in hell shall wreke their wrath." (Act IV, sc. 1)

Elizabeth, with more cause to curse Richard but "less spirit" to do it, says "Amen." She follows the Duchess, but Richard asks to have a word with her. Instinctively, Elizabeth believes he means more harm to her family. When she learns it is her daughter Elizabeth he wants to marry, she vehemently denounces the idea. If necessary, she will swear that she is illegitimate and not Edward's daughter.

Like the wooing of Lady Anne (Act I, sc. 1) Richard is repulsed by Elizabeth at every promise he makes and every explanation of his cruelty to her family. When he asks her how he might best woo her daughter Elizabeth mocks him. She suggests sending a letter with "a pair of bleeding hearts" engraved "Edward and York"; a handkerchief that he could say had been dipped in their blood to wipe her eyes.

But Richard is patient. In a long speech he describes how she can live again in honor and happiness through her daughter as Queen. He cannot recall the dead, but he can make her again mother of a King and "the ruins of distrustful times/ Repair'd with double riches of content." And he bids her, "Go, then, my mother, to thy daughter go." Elizabeth must prepare her for marriage, and when he has chastised "dull-brain'd Buckingham," he will marry her. Then "she shall be sole victress, Caesar's Caesar."

Elizabeth tantalizes him with her questions and objections. She loses no opportunity to taunt him for the children "Thou hast butcher'd." After a long speech promising "to prosper and repent," he calls on heaven and fortune to refuse him happy hours and the planets of good luck to oppose him if his love for Elizabeth's daughter is not a holy love. His final plea shows how desolation and ruin to the nation will be avoided by his marriage to her daughter.

Elizabeth, questioning herself is she can be so tempted by the devil, leaves, promising to win her daughter for Richard. As she goes, she utters a last reproach for his murder of her children. Accepting Richard's "true love's kiss" for her daughter, she states that he must write to her "very shortly," and she will give her daughter's answer.

Comment

Sixteenth century chronicles give this scene substance. They are caustic in commenting on Elizabeth's willingness to give her daughter to Richard. But it is more likely that she either fooled him or Lord Stanley prevailed on her to urge her daughter to accept Richmond.

If Elizabeth is deceiving Richard, he seems unaware of it. To him she is a "Relenting fool, and shallow-changing woman!" He turns immediately to the news brought by Ratcliff and Catesby. A "puissant navy" has been seen on the west coast. It is reported that Richmond is the Admiral.

Richard tells Catesby to go immediately to the Duke of Norfolk; but, as if dazed for a moment, he forgets to give him the message. He quickly remembers. Catesby is to tell Norfolk to meet him at Salisbury with the "greatest strength and power he can make." Richard confuses a command to Rutland. When the latter complains that he has been given no errand Richard remarks, "My mind is changed." He turns abruptly to greet Stanley who has just entered the room.

Stanley's news is not good. He is twitted by Richard for delay in telling it. In a blunt statement he reveals that "Richmond is on the seas."

Comment

The situation at the moment is extremely perilous for Stanley, actually an ally of Richmond. He knows Richard distrusts him and is gambling that he can outwit him.

Richard hopes Richmond is a victim of the seas. He asks what the "white-liver'd renegate" is up to. Stanley can only "guess." Pressed for his "guess" Stanley replies, "Stirr'd up by Dorset, Buckingham and Ely,/ He makes for England, here, to claim the Crown."

Stanley's blunt "guess" roils Richard, and he tosses a string of questions at Stanley: "Is the King dead? the empire unpossess'd?/ What heir of York is there alive but we?/ And who is England's King?" Why should Richmond be on the sea? Unless it is that he wants to be King, Stanley "cannot guess."

Richard snarls, "Unless for that he comes to be your liege." He fears Stanley will revolt and aid Richmond. Firmly denying that he would be disloyal. Stanley can, however, offer no immediate army. The reason he gives is that his "friends are in the north." If given leave to go there, Stanley will "muster" them and meet Richard when and where it pleases him. But Richard refuses to trust him, despite Stanley's avowal that he has never had cause to find him disloyal: that he "never was nor never will be."

It is arranged that Stanley can leave, but Richard demands his son, George Stanley, as a hostage. And he warns, "look your faith be firm,/ Or else his head's assurance is but frail." Stanley's parting remark. "So deal with him, as I prove true to you" is equivocal, but Richard is too engrossed to notice it.

Comment

Has Stanley done wrong in lying to Richard that he will be loyal? Is Stanley a traitor in lying to his King? Can his action be condoned on the grounds that he acts for the good of the nation? Is Richard mentally irresponsible? Shakespeare has given Stanley no occasion to answer these questions.

Richard is beset by messengers, each bringing news of uprisings. Sir Edward Courtney of Devonshire, with his brother the Bishop of Exeter, is in arms; the Guildfords in Kent have raised an army and are moving against him; Buckingham's army is marching. Deeply disturbed, Richard orders the messengers to leave - "Out on ye, owls!" who have only "songs of death." He interrupts the third messenger and strikes him, "take thou that, till thou bring better news." But his message is good: Buckingham's troops have been scattered and he has fled alone. Richard begs pardon for the blow and tosses his purse to the messenger. He learns that word has already been given to capture Buckingham.

The fourth messenger brings news that Lovel and Dorset are heading an army in Yorkshire. He also says that Richmond's fleet has been dispersed by storms: the Commander doubted the loyalty of the army ashore that claimed to follow Buckingham and now the fleet is sailing back to France.

Richard commands his train to "March on," but halts when Catesby arrives with the word that Buckingham has been captured. He contradicts the news of Richmond's fleet. The young Admiral has landed "a mighty power" in Milford Haven. Immediately Richard with his troops starts for Salisbury, and gives an order that Buckingham is to be brought there.

SUMMARY

As this long scene opens, it serves as a kind of Greek chorus heralding the triumphs of Nemesis:

1. Queen Margaret, Cassandra-like and deranged, a victim of her own crimes, the last of the Lancastrians, exults in the revenge Nemesis has already wrought. "And now I cloy me with beholding it." With almost sadistic glee she tells off the names of Richard's noble henchmen who are "Untimely smother'd in their dusky graves."

2. Opposed to Margaret is the old Duchess of York, representing the House of York, its triumphs and its failure. The abuse Margaret heaps on her as the Mother of Richard arouses sympathy for her. She is the one character in the play who is not involved in any of the political schemes that threaten the English throne. Her great moment comes when she meets Richard, and distraught by Margaret's taunts she

turns on him and face-to-face delivers her "heavy curse." Embodied in the curse is the exact and tragic end of Richard.

3. Elizabeth, as Queen of Edward IV, has a particular function other than to bemoan the death of her young children, and through their tragedy become another victim of Nemesis for assenting to the death of Clarence. His children were the first to taunt her (Act II, sc. 2) for her lack of sympathy on the death of their father.

Richard's wooing of Elizabeth to gain her daughter parallels his wooing of Anne. It is Elizabeth's first meeting with Richard since the murder of her children. The fatal fascination that he can exercise over his victims apparently subdues her.

4. The first signs of Richard's mental breakdown come immediately after his triumph with Elizabeth. He has a lapse of memory; he changes his mind; he foolishly asks why Richmond should "claim the crown" - England has a King.

5. The position of Stanley as a supporter of Richard now shifts surreptitiously to Richmond. This intrigue serves to give an element of suspense. It also starts a precipitous descent of the action of the plot in order to increase the effect of the multiple misfortunes that are steadily belaboring Richard.

6. Catesby's news that Buckingham is taken gives Richard a momentary respite from Nemesis, but he is soon plunged in deeper gloom when he learns Richmond has landed "a mighty power" on England's

> shore. Richard does not appear after this scene until we meet him on Bosworth Field. It is here that his mother's prophecy, "Bloody will be thy end," will be fulfilled.

ACT IV: SCENE 5

This scene takes place in Lord Stanley's house. It is scarcely more than a short conversation between him and Sir Christopher Urswick.

Since his son George is held by Richard as a hostage. Stanley's position at the Court is extremely precarious. He is anxious that Richmond understand the situation. Except for the danger to his son. Stanley would send Richmond aid immediately.

Urswick tells him that Richmond is either at Pembroke, or in nearby Haverford West in Wales. He satisfies Stanley that men of "noble fame and worth" are aiding Richmond. All the troops of his allies are now on their way to London, unless stopped by battle. Without comment Stanley gives Urswick letters for Richmond that will "resolve him of my mind." He sends greetings to Richmond, also the Queen's word that her daughter, Elizabeth, will marry Richmond.

SUMMARY

> This scene is necessary to set Stanley apart from the self-seeking nobles that have served at Richard's Court. His avowal of Richmond's cause is not based on the selfish motive to have his family on the English throne. Stanley sees Richard as "the most bloody boar" leading the nation into civil war.

This scene serves the following purposes:

1. The contents of the letters which Stanley gives Urswick for Richmond are not divulged. Later (Act V, sc. 2) Richmond mentions receiving from "our father Stanley/ Lines of fair comfort and encouragement."

2. Elizabeth's word that her daughter is to marry Richmond is safer if sent verbally. So Urswick is to "tell him."

3. The scene suggests that the renowned men of the nation have awakened to the fact that Richard is "mad". Stanley is one of them who knows well that Richard will not take advice. We have heard him say to his mother (Act IV, sc. 4), "Madam, I have a touch of your condition,/ That cannot brook the accent of reproof."

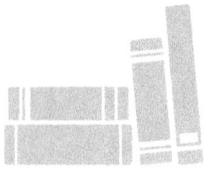

RICHARD III

TEXTUAL ANALYSIS

ACT V

ACT V: SCENE 1

This scene takes place in an open space in Salisbury.

Buckingham is led to execution by the Sheriff and a guard. The scene is almost a soliloquy interrupted twice by short retorts from the Sheriff.

Buckingham has asked to speak with Richard, but the request has been denied. He tells of Richard's victims, mentioning Hastings first. If those "moody, discontented souls" are peering at him through the clouds and mocking him-Buckingham doesn't finish. He remembers it is All Souls Day.

Comment

Historically, Buckingham was executed on All Saints Day (November 1st, 1843), the day that precedes All Souls Day.

It was this day, years before in the time of King Edward IV, that he wished would mark his death if he were found disloyal to Edward or "False to his children or his wife's allies." He recognizes he "dallied" with God who has turned his "feigned prayer" on his head and given him what he "begg'd in jest." So man uses his free will to punish himself. Margaret's curse (Act I, sc. 3) comes vividly to Buckingham's mind. He quotes her words; Richard "shall split thy heart with sorrow." Now he can say "Margaret was a prophetess." He asks to be led to execution, moralizing as he goes that wrong begets wrong and "blame the due of blame."

SUMMARY

This scene gives the tragic end of Buckingham, the last of Richard's victims. He is the most callous among the nobles who played Richard's game of bloody usurpation. Buckingham realizes too late the vital mistakes he made:

1. He jibed at Hastings when, full of confidence, he went to meet Richard in the Tower.

2. He was false to his oath to be loyal to Edward IV's children and allies.

3. He paid no attention to Margaret's dire warnings of Richard's treachery.

Buckingham expresses no sorrow for what he has done, neither dallying with God nor abetting Richard's murders. He has a moral blindness that shuts out eternal values.

ACT V: SCENE 2

This scene takes place on a plain near Tamworth. Like the preceding two scenes, it is almost a soliloquy by Richmond. Accompanied by the Earl of Oxford, Sir James Blunt, Sir Walter Herbert, and others, Richmond appears in the play for the first time.

Comment

Shakespeare has drawn on Holinshed's description of the boy Richmond visiting Henry VI. The King remarked, "Lo, surelie this is he, to whom both we and our adversaries, leaving the possession of all things, shall hereafter give room and place." Holinshed remarks that Richmond never forgot the prophecy and was always grateful to Henry VI.

His address to his forces is a sincere plea for loyalty. He bases their allegiance to him on the necessity to rid themselves from the "yoke of tyranny" imposed by Richard, the "wretched, bloody and usurping boar." Richmond tells of the comfort and support he is promised by his father, Stanley (Act IV, sc. 5). Word is brought that Richard and his troops are near Leicester, a day's march away. With one battle they can "reap the harvest of perpetual peace." Each of Richmond's friends offers a word of encouragement: they are fighting against "bloody homicide" in an honest cause; Richard's friends are bound to him by fear; in the hour of need they will forsake him.

Richmond closes the scene exhorting them to march "In God's name." He declares that "true hope is swift." It reduces kings to idols and makes "meaner creatures kings."

SUMMARY

This short scene serves to introduce Richmond and disclose the characters of the nobles who accompany him. As a leader, it can be said of Richmond:

1. He appears to be upright and stalwart. He is eager to overthrow Richard's tyrannical hold on the nation.

2. He warns his troops that liberation of the English people depends on their courage and loyalty.

3. He exhorts them in God's name to march and keep their hopes high.

The men who are supporting Richmond express the same sentiments:

1. Oxford makes his plea on the force of each man's conscience to fight against homicide.

2. Herbert believes Richard has only fickle friends.

3. Blunt touches the vulnerable point in Richard's drive for success. Richard has no friends except those who follow him through fear. In his "dearest need" they will desert him.

ACT V: SCENE 3

This scene is laid on Bosworth Field, a battle ground near Liecester in central England. (Shakespeare disregards the actual date of the battle, August 22, 1485.) It is evening. Richard's troops are encamped on one end of the field, and Richmond's troops at the other. The action shifts from camp to camp.

Richard enters with his troops, accompanied by the Duke of Norfolk, the Earl of Surrey, and others. Orders are given to pitch his tent. He banters with Surrey and Norfolk, complaining the former looks sad; agreeing with the latter that they must give and take. Norfolk advices Richard that their opponents' power numbers "six or seven thousand."

Comment

The size of Richard's forces is said to have numbered about 12,000. Richmond has less than half that number. The forces that Lord Stanley brought into the battle at its height gave Richmond the strength needed to win.

Three times as many are fighting for Richard, who remarks "Besides, the King's name is a tower of strength." After taking every precaution for success by ordering men recognized for their military skill to survey the battle ground, Richard leaves with Norfolk and Surrey.

The action shifts immediately to Richmond's camp. He enters with Sir William Brandon, Oxford, and others. Soldiers are readying his tent.

Richmond comments on the sunset as predicting fair weather. He appoints Brandon as his standard bearer. Then calling for ink and paper, he will begin to sketch the plan of battle and assign each leader his particular duty. All the nobles leave except Oxford, Brandon, Herbert and Blunt, who remain for consultation.

Blunt is sent to tell the Earl of Pembroke to visit Richmond at "the second hour in the morning." He is also to deliver a letter to his step-father, Lord Stanley, whose forces are encamped a half mile away. With his leaders, Richmond enters his tent to plan the next day's battle.

In Richard's tent he talks with Norfolk, Ratcliff, Catesby and others. It is nine o'clock and "supper-time," but Richard will not dine. He is anxious about his armor.

Norfolk is bid goodnight and told to "stir with the lark tomorrow." Catesby is sent to Lord Stanley who must bring his troops before sunrise or his son, George, will forfeit his head. Richard's attendants bring him wine and a "watch," as he demands.

Comment

"Watch" is not to be understood to mean a sentry. It was most likely a night candle. The markings on the candle indicated the hours so that it served the purpose of the modern watch.

His horse, Surrey, must be readied for the field. Ratcliff allays his fears about the "melancholy Lord Northumberland": with the Earl of Surrey he has been "cheering up the soldiers." Richard asks for another bowl of wine, and complains that he has not the "cheer of mind" that he was wont to have. Ratcliff has procured ink and paper for him, and is told to return at midnight to help Richard arm. Richard retires alone into his tent and sleeps.

We return now to Richmond's tent. He is seen talking with his officers as Lord Stanley enters. Richmond greets him warmly as his "noble father-in-law."

Comment

An interesting comparison can be made between the attitudes toward their sons of the mothers, Margaret Beaufort, Richmond's mother, and the Duchess of York, the mother of Richard.

Stanley brings greetings from Richmond's mother and tells of her prayers for him. It is a brief visit. He advices Richmond to fight a "mortal-staring war." He cannot shift his troops immediately to Richmond's side because his young son, George Stanley (Richmond's stepbrother), would be executed by Richard "in his father's sight." Expressing a fond farewell, Stanley leaves. Richmond sends his officers as an escort to see him safely to his regiment.

Richmond says that he will try "to take a nap." When all have left, before he retires, Richmond prays that God "whose captain I account myself" will look on his cause with a gracious eye. And "sleeping and waking," he asks for divine protection.

Both Richard and Richmond retire for the night. While Richard sleeps, he has a troubled dream.

Comment

According to Holinshed's Chronicle Richard had "a terrible dream" the night before the battle. He saw "diverse images like terrible divels which pulled and haled him" so that he had no rest. Richard interpreted the dream as a bad omen.

In the center of the field between their tents there arise, one by one, ten ghosts, the souls of those whom Richard has murdered. Prince Edward, son of Henry VI, is the first. The others follow in the order of their demise. Each ghost speaks to him, identifies itself and accuses him of its murder. The last word of each is almost the same, "despair and die!" As each of the ghosts leaves Richard, it appears to Richmond bidding him, "live thou, and flourish!"

Richard awakens from his dream startled. He thinks he has lost his horse, and asks that his wounds be bound up. When he realizes that he has been dreaming, he upbraids his "coward conscience," aroused at long last, for so afflicting him. The candle burns blue so he knows it is midnight.

Comment

This is the second time in the play that Shakespeare has used a dream, filled with terror, to precede the character's death. (Compare Clarence's dream in Act I, sc. 4.)

In a long soliloquy Richard reveals a tortured mind looking at itself-one moment he condemns himself for his crimes and the next, proclaims "Richard loves Richard." But his conscience "has a thousand several tongues." Each tongue accuses him at eternity's court and cries "Guilty! guilty!" No one loves him, no one will ever pity him. Despairing, he should have no pity because he exclaims, "I myself/ Find in myself no pity to myself."

Ratcliff interrupts him to say his friends are buckling on their armor. Richard confides the details of his "fearful dream" to Ratcliff. The terror they roused in him was greater than ten thousand troops fighting against him under "shallow Richmond." He leaves with Ratcliff to go eavesdropping around the soldiers' tents to find if they are disloyal to him.

Richmond is awakened in his tent by Oxford and other lords. He tells them he has had "The sweetest sleep, and fairest-boding dreams." He thought that the souls "whose bodies Richard murder'd" came to his tent and cried, "On! victory!" His heart is "very jocund." When he discovers it is four in the morning, Richmond remarks "then 'tis time to arm and give direction."

Richmond advances toward his troops and addresses them as "loving countrymen." He asks them to remember their cause is good and God is on their side, as are the saints and the wronged souls. He describes Richard's tyrannical climb to the throne. His deeds proclaim him God's enemy and He "will, in justice, ward you as His soldiers;/ If you do sweat to put a tyrant down." Richmond's speech rises to a **climax** as he proclaims the spiritual and material benefits their victory will bring to their country, wives, and children. If Richmond wins they will share his glory.

The scene changes to Richard's sector of the field. He talks with Ratcliff, who brings reports from Northumberland and Surrey. The first belittles Richmond as he "was never train'd up in arms"; the latter considers that a boon. Richard is satisfied with the report. The weather is dull, and he believes it a bad omen; "A black day will it be to somebody."

Norfolk enters with the news that the foe is already in the field. Richard calls for his horse. He commands that Lord Stanley's forces be brought up. The general plan of the battle, as he has sketched it, is disclosed by Richard to Norfolk and Surrey. They will command the "Foot and Horse,' and Richard will follow in "the main battle."

Norfolk commends Richard's plan. Casually, he shows him a scroll that he found "on his tent." Richard reads the **rhyme**:

"Jockey of Norfolk, be not too bold,/ For Dickon thy master is bought and sold."

Comment

Jockey and Dickon were nicknames for John and Richard. The message "bought and sold" infers a treacherous deal has been made involving Richard. It has the sound of an old proverb.

Richard, aware of the traitorous meaning, declares it was "devised by the enemy." He urges his leaders to victory and cautions them not to be disturbed by "babbling dreams," nor by conscience, a coward's word. "Our strong arms be our conscience, swords our law."

Richard turns to address his soldiers. In a long speech he does little else than disparage Richmond and his troops - "A sort of vagabonds, rascals, and runaways." They are the "scum of Bretagne" who are vomited forth to seek venture and destruction. Richmond, he claims, is a "paltry fellow" and "a milk-sop" who has been held a political refugee in France.

Comment

Richmond was held in custody in France by Richard's brother-in-law, Charles, Duke of Burgundy. The name "milk-sop" is used by both Hall and Holinshed to describe Richmond. Each mentions his lack of training in war.

As Richard finishes his talk, the sound of drums is heard, and he again exhorts his men to victory. A messenger hurries in to say that Stanley refuses to bring up his troops. Richard immediately orders Stanley's son, George, beheaded. Norfolk suggests he wait - the battle is more important at the moment as the enemy has crossed the marsh. At once, Richard commands his troops to advance and fight "like fiery dragons." With the war cry, "Victory sits on our helms," they march into battle.

SUMMARY

This scene is one of the most exciting in the play. It is good theatre and affords an interesting psychological approach in the handling of the revenge theme:

1. It highlights the differences in character between Richard and Richmond. Shakespeare has made Richard a thoroughly evil villain; Richmond, a young, upright, virtuous leader.

2. The close proximity of the tents of the two leaders was the only alternative in presenting the ghosts so that the audience could make a quick appraisal of each leader as the action shifts back and forth.

3. It contains the most vital event in the play as it, finally, makes Richard a victim of Nemesis. At the end Fate is tantalizingly brutal with Richard, giving him some hope (when Buckingham is repulsed and caught), then plunging him into despair (news that Richmond had landed). Finally, Stanley rebels.

When Richard orders some wine to encourage sleep, instead of rest, it brings a hideous dream. If awake, his will would be free, and he could banish dreams, but asleep he has become his own victim. After the dream Richard is mentally and physically weakened. Now he is clearly on the defensive-a role that has come too suddenly for him to master. Before this he could reason his way out of problems, but now remorse plagues every effort he makes to win.

4. His speech to his soldiers, unlike Richmond's courageous appeal, is only a frenzied piece of venom.

5. When Richard goes off to battle, he is a phantom of his former self. He is buoyed up by false hope, but the old **rhyme** is ringing in his ear: "Dickon . . . is bought and sold."

ACT V: SCENE 4

This brief scene takes place in another part of the field. Norfolk enters leading his troops. Catesby hurries on stage to tell him of Richard's plight - his horse has been killed, and he is fighting on foot. He races about looking for Richmond.

Richard enters calling for a horse. Catesby offers to help him. Crazed with the desire to kill Richmond, he declares he has already killed five men, mistaking each for Richmond. Offering his kingdom for a horse, he goes back to the field of battle.

SUMMARY

The scene is almost a sketch of Richard a few moments before his death. Broken in mind and body, with only a wisp of his indomitable will forcing him on, he is a pathetic figure. He knows that he is beaten, and the knowledge heightens the tragedy. Fortune has played him false: he gained the crown, now, in order to keep it, he offers to give it away to gain the means to win it back-a vicious circle. Remorse of conscience

> plagues him. Like the Marlovian hero that he is, Richard, without sorrow or contrition for his crimes, staggers off to enter his last combat.

ACT V: SCENE 5

This scene follows immediately. Richard and Richmond enter from opposite sides of the stage and engage in a duel. They continue fighting as they move off stage, and Richard is slain.

Richmond returns to give "God and your arms" praise for the victory. Then he announces (curiously enough, in Margaret's terms, see Act IV, sc. 4) "the bloody dog is dead."

Stanley is the first to congratulate him. He has taken the crown from Richard's head and places it on Richmond, telling him to "Wear it, enjoy it, and make much of it." Richmond is grateful when he learns George Stanley's life has been spared. He orders that the nobles who were slain on Richard's side be given burial "as becomes their births." He proclaims a general pardon for deserters who fought for Richard, provided they submit to his rule.

When he has received the Sacrament he will wed Elizabeth and so "unite the white rose and the red." His last address to his troops laments the scars left on England by the long civil war. It made enemies of brothers, fathers, and sons.

He hopes the union of the Houses of Lancaster and York will bring peace. He calls "Richmond and Elizabeth,/ The true succeeders of each royal House." He hopes God will bless them with issue and secure the future with "smooth-faced peace." He hails the end of war - now "peace lives again:/ That she may long live here, God say Amen!"

SUMMARY

This scene as a finale does the following things:

1. It gives a first impression of Richmond as King-God-fearing, fair, compassionate, honest.

2. Though Stanley has dissembled with Richard, his remarks to Richmond and the defection of his troops to the Duke indicate that he knows he is dealing with an insane despot. In this way he justifies his actions.

3. Through the coming marriage of Richard and Elizabeth England is promised peace - that peace to which Richard paid tribute in his opening soliloquy, then willfully shattered.

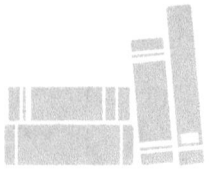

RICHARD III

CHARACTER ANALYSES

In presenting an analysis of the characters who take part in *King Richard The Third*, it is necessary to point out that each of them has appeared and lived a lifetime, so to speak, in the three parts of *King Henry, VI*. Now there remains, in King Richard, only the exciting business of winding up their affairs and sending them one by one packing off to eternity. Most of them go as victims of the same cruel knife they themselves wielded on an enemy. Richard, Duke of Gloucester, later King Richard III, is the chief executioner for Nemesis. Then, after eight slayings, his own turn on the block comes, and the final curtain descends on one of the greatest Senecan revenge plays in English drama.

KING RICHARD

Richard, the little crook-backed dictator, is a symbol of fear to all around him. The product of a misguided youth, Richard grew into manhood hating the world because he believed the world hated him. He was born only "half made up." Constantly aware of his deformities, his personality has become soured and warped. Now, in his prime, the only persons for whom he has the slightest respect are his parents-his "princely father," Richard, Duke of York, and his aged mother, the Duchess of York, although she never shows the slightest affection for him. His deformity may have so embittered her that she hated the sight of him. The grim sketch of his life that she gives him is bitter and humiliating before those about him. He listens, but makes no reply. She was naturally proud and he embarrassed her. There was no help for it. Might it be that the strange wooing scenes are done to prove he could win a woman? In each case the woman was a political convenience, but he mustered a love jargon with Anne and Elizabeth that finally subdued them. Richard has a keen mind and a strong physique that his deformity has not weakened. When the idea of becoming King enters his mind, it soon becomes an obsession, and he moves toward it like an arrow shot from a bow. Shakespeare shows no growth or change in Richard. From the beginning of his mad march to the throne, he enjoys villainy. Conscience is his first victim. He can call on God to revenge his enemies, but His laws can have no place in his scheme for power. With all the qualities of a Marlovian figure, Richard has one that is lacking in Faustus and *Tamburlaine*. He has a sense of humor, sardonic though it is. It lightens up "asides," and the mock-attack by an enemy that he stages to impress the Lord Mayor is a hilarious bit of foolery that actually makes a point. But Richard can gamble only so far with Nemesis. Eight victims and more (King Henry VI and his heir, Prince Edward) bring him to the throne but also to the bar of reckoning. It is a peculiar twist of Nemesis that Richard should go into the battle at Bosworth Field determined that he would personally kill young Richmond. Almost his last words in the play are a frustrated cry, "I think there be six Richmonds in the field;/ Five I have slain today instead of him." When he falls by Richmond's sword, it is not the death of a tragic hero; he goes weighted down with the curse of the living and of his victims from the other world. It is only Shakespeare's art that can turn Richard's arch villainy into a symbol of evil.

KING EDWARD THE FOURTH

We get only a quick glance at this ill and senile oldest son of Richard, Duke of York. Always a weak ruler, Edward, now a gullible and tottering old man, allows himself to be used as a tool by Richard. He believes in "dreams, drunken prophecies and libels." Aware of his weakness, Richard wheedles a death warrant out of him for their brother, Clarence: afraid of losing his throne to the latter's treachery, Edward issues the warrant. This very instrument, intended to thwart any danger to the throne, ironically causes the stroke that kills him. True, Edward does rescind the warrant, but the "countermand" comes too late. We see him practically on his death bed trying, again too late, to make peace among his family and the nobles at his court. When he is interrupted by Lord Stanley who begs the King's mercy for a servant, he launches into a long speech filled with self pity. Mercy is the one power Edward now has left, yet it is too late to exercise it to save the brother he unjustly condemned. He leaves the stage to die an embittered, disillusioned old man.

DUKE OF CLARENCE

The plight of Clarence, the third brother of the House of York, begets sympathy though he waded in the blood of the Lancasters when he helped usurp the throne for his brother Edward. He lacks the vigorous mentality of his brothers. And it is only when he tells his dream to the jailor that he realizes the evil that he has done. Now "mew'd up" in the Tower, he becomes frantic at the thought of dying. His plea to his murderers and his prayer to God to spare his wife and children are the last pathetic whimpers of one who basked in the spoils of a gory victory and forgot that the price for it is always in the same terms, that is to say, death.

PRINCE EDWARD (EDWARD V) AND THE DUKE OF YORK

Young Prince Edward (King Edward V) and his brother, the Duke of York, are delightful youngsters. Edward takes his position very seriously. The simple trust each has in Richard points up his diabolical scheming. He seems to enjoy bantering with the young Duke, perhaps he is even proud of his namesake's wit. Their instinctive dislike for staying in the Tower is predicated on murder, especially of their Uncle Clarence. There might be ghosts! The last little speech of the young Prince, bravely going off to the Tower "with a heavy heart," arouses more hatred for Richard than Margaret's litany of his crimes.

EARL OF RICHMOND

He is the one character in the play who is completely removed from the powers of Nemesis. He is a force for good and for peace. His brief appearance is, however, sufficient to establish him as the antithesis of the evil Richard: he is youthful, kind, and full of piety; his relations with his mother and stepfather, Lord Stanley, are warm and friendly; his troops are "fellows in arms" and his "most loving friends." Richmond's reward for good comes not only from his earthly relatives and friends, but, also, in the "blessing" of the ghosts. He interprets the "dream" as a prophecy of victory, and it raises his spirits. As Richmond is never seen except under great pressure, it is not possible to say more than that he is a just man and a thinker. He enters the play resolved to defeat Richard and goes about it without hysteria. When the battle is won, he announces simply that Richard is dead. He is quick to praise God for His help and his men as "victorious friends." Contrary to Richard, he wears his laurels easily. Lord Stanley calls him courageous when he places on his head Richard's crown. Unlike Richard, he makes no tests of loyalty to the Crown. Rather, Richmond grants a general amnesty to the soldiers who fought against him, provided they will submit to his rule. Again contrary to Richard, Richmond considers marriage as a solemn and lasting bond. With no time for wooing, he announces simply that "after he has taken the Sacrament/ We will unite the white rose and red." Richard is not mentioned by name in his long address, of which the keynotes is peace through union. Richmond and Elizabeth by the will of God will be united and bring "smooth faced peace" to live long in England.

LORD STANLEY

Stanley is a quiet man with comparatively little to say. He is a thinker and also a kind man. When he rushes in to beg King Edward IV to save a servant from execution, the incident reveals much about him. It is true in his case that still waters run deep. Stanley, who will finally solve the bloody riddle that Richard makes of himself, is the most silent character in the play. As such, he is a foil for the talkative, unprincipled Buckingham. Behind the scenes he works to undermine the King. This is a traitorous act, but is Richard a legitimate successor of his brother Edward, or an usurper? Much hangs on the answer. Evidently, Stanley has the good of the nation at heart when, on the eve of battle, he lies to Richard about his absolute fealty to the Crown. But the end does not justify the means. Can we surmise that Stanley looked on Richard as a usurper and insane, and was pricked by conscience to do what lay in his power to dethrone him? As a man of great wealth and high rank he did not need to seek preferment by having his stepson, Richmond, on the throne.

DUKE OF BUCKINGHAM

Buckingham tries valiantly to keep step with Richard in his parade of evil. Unlike Stanley, Buckingham wants honors and wealth for his pains. It might be said Buckingham is Richard's lackey in crime. In the beginning nothing is too large, nothing is too small, for him to do if it will help Richard attain the Crown. He readily begs "God punish me" if he is ever false to the Queen. Then he stands ready to help Richard plot against her and her family. Caught in Nemesis' net, the promise returns to plague his as he goes to his execution. But meantime Richard finds him a handy tool-he could nicely ferret out a "traitor" like Hastings; he can "play" at war games; harangue the citizens to accepts his master as king; and then assist him up the steps of the throne. But Richard knew his underlings. It is his promise to give Buckingham an earldom and the late King's "moveable" that is goading him on. Unlike Stanley, Buckingham believes Richard-more than that, he believes there is give-and-take with him. When Buckingham pauses to consider and then discuss the murder of the young princes, he signs his own death warrant. On the way to the "block" he remembers, "Margaret was a prophetess," as she said.

LORD HASTINGS

Hastings is not so quick witted as Buckingham, and so less useful to Richard. His term in the Tower taught him little. He is arrogant and over confident in himself, qualities which spring from an imagined friendship with Richard. The bond between them is hatred for the Queen and her family. Stanley attempts to alert Hastings to Richard's treachery. Hastings jests at his fears about the "boar." He believes he is invulnerable now and that his enemies are being readied for Nemesis' shroud. Revenge exhilarates him to the point where he rashly flaunts his opinion to a menial sent by Richard to get his views on the Protector's assuming the English Crown. Like Buckingham, he pays bitterly for the tugs of conscience that prompt loyalty to Edward's children. It is difficult to overlook the coincidence that the Queen's brother and son are paying Nemesis' debt in Wales (for "standing by when Richard stabb'd" Queen Margaret's son) while Hastings, who helped them to the block, steps jauntily along unknowingly to meet his doom. Like the others, he remembers Margaret's "heavy curse" on him. Despite the impatience of his executioner, he has his say on the folly by seeking favors from men rather than from God.

THE DUCHESS OF YORK

As the mother of the three Yorkists, King Edward, George, Duke of Clarence, and Richard, Duke of Gloucester and King, she is looked on as a high born noblewoman of her day. She reflects the harshness of the times in her contempt for her deformed son. As the representative of the House of York, she realizes that the bloodshed caused by her sons' bitter antagonism toward the Lancasters makes her the "mother of these moans." When we see her, she is an embittered old woman trying, too late, to use her influence for good on Richard. It would seem that Shakespeare is pointing, an accusing finger at her for her complete lack of understanding of Richard and his severe physical handicap. When she questions Margaret and Elizabeth why calamity should be so full of words, Elizabeth tells her they help "ease the heart." She is eager to try it. When Richard passes by her at the head of his troops her parental tongue-lashing is scarcely matched in all literature. Richard listens but makes no reply. Is he callous? Has her shame and contempt for him as a young child helped to make him indifferent? It is typical of her to be affectionate to her good looking and winsome grandchildren. At an earlier meeting with her, Richard showed respect for his mother. However, her remarks have always been tinged with bitterness. Earlier, he jests at her pious admonitions. Does he do it to make light of her public scolding? Richard might have gotten even with her and told the public the questionable rumor that Edward was her bastard son. But he warned Buckingham to say little about it, "Because, my lord, you know my mother lives." On the other hand, would it reflect on him? In this she is a creature of her times, doling out sympathy and kindness when it is easy, but unable and unwilling to bear misfortunes that all human beings are heir to. With the two Queens, Margaret and Elizabeth, she stands as a pathetic figure while Nemesis scoffs at her, "a poor moral living ghost."

QUEEN ELIZABETH

It could be considered a left-handed compliment that Richard describes her as "subtle." She outwitted him in her marriage to Edward. He tried to undermine her reputation by linking her name with the notorious Mistress Shore. But he never succeeded in turning Edward or the court against her. If she lent her prestige as Queen of the imprisonment of Clarence, it is her only fault. It is extremely doubtful that she encouraged Edward to sign a warrant for his brother's execution. She declares her life as Queen has been unhappy and, in the play, she moves from one tragedy to another - the death of Edward, the beheading of her brother, Lord Rivers, and of her elder son, Lord Grey, and the murder of her two young sons in the Tower. There is scarcely a more moving scene in the play than when Elizabeth, forbidden to see her children in the Tower, turns to go, then pauses to look back. In her fear, she calls to the old stone building "rude ragged nurse" and "old sullen play-fellow" to use her "babies well." If ever she outwitted Richard it was in duping him that she would encourage her daughter to marry him. There is no hint in her character throughout the play to suggest her approval of an incestuous union between her daughter and Richard. By pretending to agree with him, she gained time to take her daughter safely out of his reach. It can be said of her: she is more sinned against than sinning.

LADY ANNE

Anne is a charming and beautiful young widow, if Richard's word can be trusted. A victim of circumstances, she is caught in Nemesis' net. Unlike others, it is not her sin but the sins of her father, Duke of Warwick, who deserted the Yorkists, that are visited on her. So she is bait for Richard. And with the irresistible fascination that he exercises over men and women alike, she is helpless to overcome him. Her bitter denunciation of him as the vilest of murderers only feeds his desire to possess her . . . not for love, but for the Warwick fortune she inherited. Intuitively, she knows he will soon dispose of her. It is scarcely a year before she "bids the world good night." We get a final glimpse of her as she goes to her coronation. When she stops to talk with the Duchess and Queen Elizabeth, neither interrupts her. Anne seems to know that her coronation is the beginning of the end: "Besides, he hates me because of my father Warwick;/ And will, no doubt, shortly be rid of me." And word for word she repeats her long curse, in substance "the miserable life" she had wished, the day she met Richard, for the woman who married him. Now the curse has come back to plague her. Unsung and unmourned, Anne goes off to join the coterie of Richard's victims.

QUEEN MARGARET

As the Duchess represents the House of York, so Margaret, the Queen of Henry VI, represents the House of Lancaster. A woman of dynamic personality-a leader of armies and an executioner of enemies-she has brought herself now to the brink of insanity by constantly bewailing the lost cause of the Lancastrians. In this play (she appears in the 3 parts of *Henry VI*), she is a shadow of her former self, condemned, as it were, to play Nemesis, a union of sin and punishment. As such she comes unbidden to a group of Yorkists gathered in the palace to discuss King Edward's health. She listens to their bickering. She seizes her chance and spews forth venomous curses on each of them for their murders. It does not harass her that they call her "a lunatic." She knows she will win. And it is scarcely a year before she gloats over the tragic deaths that she prophesied. Now she has witnessed the slaying of the Yorkists. One is left-Richard. He had killed her husband and her son. With that curious renaissance blending of paganism with the Judeo and Christian theologies, she begs the fiends of hell and the saints of heaven to ask God to kill him. She will be ready for her own requiem if He will let her live to say. "The dog is dead." As a forceful Nemesis, Margaret is a worthy descendant of Clytemnestra, Medea, and Videna of Gorboduc.

MINOR CHARACTERS

As the Queen's brother, Rivers, more than her son, Grey, who is executed with him, becomes a symbol of Richard's hate. But he does not miss the chance to use Rivers to further his schemes against Clarence. With the Queen, Rivers assented to Clarence's imprisonment, making him responsible for his death warrant. Like Stanley, Rivers has little to say openly. The few times he meets Richard his sharp quipping antagonizes him. Richard accuses him of seeking power and prestige at court. His best moment comes in the scene with Margaret. Like the rest, he falls under her curse for idly watching the murder of her son. And like them, he has his turn on the block. His execution is Richard's first act as Lord Protector. Vaughan, though not a relative of the Queen, is executed with them because Richard distrusts his long friendship for King Edward. His only appearance is at his execution. He sums up the plight of England under Richard. "You live that shall cry woe for this hereafter."

Of the several clergy that appear in the play, Bishop Morton is the most important. As a member of Richard's Council, he is cautious in his remarks. Buckingham, he thought, would know Richard's mind better than anyone. And the "strawberry incident" is no doubt used by Richard to get Ely out of the room while he confers with Buckingham. It is after this Council meeting and the rash beheading of Hastings that Ely joins Richmond's forces. This news troubled Richard very deeply. He is the first openly to challenge his right to the Crown.

Cardinal Bouchier has a brief role. He has a quick exchange of views with Buckingham on the right of sanctuary invoked by Elizabeth for herself and her young son, Duke of York. From the friendly way he concedes the point, there can be no doubt that he is trying to avoid any rupture, between the Crown and the Church. The Archbishop of York, Thomas Rotherham, is a friend of the family of Edward IV and tries to guard Elizabeth and her young son against seizure of the child by Richard. He encourages them to take refuge in sanctuary. The Cardinal, in conceding Buckingham's point that the child has no right to claim sanctuary, nullifies the Archbishop's efforts. Sir Christopher Urswick, a priest, was chosen, most likely by Stanley, to carry messages to Richmond because he would not arouse suspicion. Also, he seems to be an honest partisan of Richmond and readily names those who will support the young leader.

Richard needs paid menials to do his bidding. Catesby is underhanded and double-dealing. He shifts his allegiance from King Edward to Richard. He is the invaluable hireling who becomes an agent for Richard's villainy and as such would be difficult to excel. Lovel and Ratcliff are of the same stamp, but less clever at their tasks. Sir Brackenbury, Keeper of the Tower, is a typical time server at the Court.

The son and daughter of Clarence appear briefly with their grandmother. Their function in the play is to complain against Queen Elizabeth for her coldness toward them on the death of their father. In their childish way they show the poison that Richard has instilled in their minds against the Queen.

Of the murderers hired by Richard, the most interesting are the two who murder Clarence. The First Murderer is hardened to his job, but the Second, who likes to philosophize, is not content with murder as a way of livelihood and suffers from pricks of conscience. Despite the humor of the scene, it is a clever dialogue on guilt complex.

The trio of murderers responsible for killing the young Princes afford a contrast. Tyrell, the "discontented gentleman," suggested by Richard's Page, starts out bravely to do his task. He seems a match for Richard's dire cruelty. But he becomes fearful of the consequences. Contrary to the first group in whom conscience arouses a revulsion toward crime, Tyrell and his villains suffer a remorse of conscience after the murder.

A point is being made by contrasting those who, despite all that crime entails, succumb to it for reward (a case in point is Buckingham), with the prudent man, who, though he may start out as an accomplice, through conscience gains the strength to avoid crime.

RICHARD III

CRITICAL COMMENTARY

KING RICHARD THE THIRD

King Richard The Third has always been one of the most popular of Shakespeare's plays. It was printed anonymously until 1605 when it was assigned to William Shakespeare and seemed safely launched on its way. How much the great actor Richard Burbage became identified with the part in Shakespeare's time is told in Bishop Richard Corbett's Certain Elegant Poems. A friend "full of ale and history" recounts a performance of the play, and when he "would have said, 'King Richard dyed,'/ And call'd, 'A horse, a horse'-he 'Burbage' cry'de."

CRITICS HAVE HEAPED ATTENTION ON RICHARD

Critics Have Heaped Attention On Richard at the expense of all other characters in the play. If he is drawn after the likeness of Marlowe's heroes he must dominate the plot and characters alike. Critics run the gamut of referring to him as "monstrosity" and "conscience stricken tyrant," to a man with an "imperial mind" and a "mystic fascination" that draws all people to him. With his expansive energy, he leaves no time for anyone else. Critics are generally satisfied to label Lade Anne as the bereaved little widow baffled by Richard's proposal. Elizabeth, Queen of Edward IV, is the vacillating weak woman who could barter her daughter, or, at least, pretend to. Hastings and Buckingham are both self-seekers. Margaret is the Cassandra.

WITH THE DELETIONS AND ALTERATIONS

With The Deletions And Alterations of Shakespeare's text which began in 1700, some of the characters were considered as choking the action of the play. The dramatist Colly Cibber was the first to take liberties in altering the text. He omitted many of the scenes and completely deleted the parts of Margaret and Clarence. To make Richard more of a fiend, he sends him eavesdropping on the murderers as they go about killing the Princes in the Tower. When Cibber's version was first presented, the censor ordered the entire first act to be omitted. He reasoned that the murder of King Henry VI, spoken of in the play, would disturb people and remind them of King James II, then in exile in France!

POPULAR AS THE PLAY WAS IN CIBBER'S VERSION

Popular As The Play Was In Cibber's Version, it was roundly trounced by the critic, Charles Gildon. Writing in 1714, he found *King Richard The Third* too diabolical for the stage, and that divine retribution is not meted out soon enough. In comparing Richard with Atreus and Medea, Gildon admits the latter two are "passionate sinners, but Richard is a deliberate murderer."

THE CALCULATED VILLAINY OF RICHARD

The Calculated Villainy Of Richard remained throughout the eighteenth century. Charlotte Lenox compliments Shakespeare because his conception of Richard is so close to his historical sources. She scolds the Poet, however, for letting Richard display valor and courage at the end so win some sympathy. Too, she considers the telescoping of years into a few hours is absurd. On this point, Henry Hudson, the American critic, differs widely: "This drawing together of the scattered events seems eminently judicious: for the plan of the drama required them to be used only as subservient to the hero's character: and it does not appear how the Poet could have ordered them better for developing in the most forcible manner his idea of that extraordinary man."

CIBBER'S VERSION WAS POPULAR

Cibber's Version Was Popular on the English stage when Samuel Johnson called *King Richard The Third* a lesser work by Shakespeare. "One of the most praised but yet I know not whether it has not happened to him as to others, to be praised most, when praise is not most deserved. That this play has scenes noble in themselves, and very well contrived to strike in the exhibition, cannot be denied. But some parts are trifling, others shocking, and some improbable." Elizabeth Griffiths, a contemporary of Dr. Johnson, considered the wooing of Lady Anne unbelievable. The twentieth century critic, Stopford Brooke, discussing the same point, explains that it is only Richard's lack of affection and conscience that makes such a thing at all possible. Brooke further remarks that Shakespeare is so carried away with his creative ability that Richard's second wooing scene, that of Elizabeth, is hypocritical to the point that it lessens the tragic elements of the play. But others have argued that the wooing of Elizabeth is one of the first signs of Richard's mental breakdown. He knows his kingdom stands on "brittle glass" unless he brings about a union of the two warring Houses. If marrying the young Elizabeth will bolster Richmond's cause, it will do the same for him. He moves towards its accomplishment with his usual rapidity and seems to win. The success bolsters his spirits. Richard suffers more from the "agony of failure than of sin."

THE WORKING OF NEMESIS

The Working Of Nemesis in *King Richard The Third* is one of the most fascinating facets of the play. Richard Moulton describes an interworking of Nemesis that shows the genius of Shakespeare in handling retribution: "These four Nemesis Actions [The first centers around Clarence; the second, the King; the third, Hastings; the fourth, Buckingham], it will be observed, are not separate trains of incidents going on side by side, they are linked together into a system, the law of which is seen to be that those who triumph in one Nemesis become the victims of the next; so that the whole suggests a chain of destruction, like that binding together the orders of brute creation which live by preying upon one another." When Clarence is murdered it is the King who signs the death warrant and Queen Elizabeth's relatives and friends who triumph. Nemesis turns her wheel and the King's death follows his victim's, which leaves the Queen's party exposed to their enemies. Hastings rejoices at their death only to be Nemesis' next victim. Buckingham, who enjoys goading the gullible Hastings into Richard's net, meets a like fate when he is trapped by Richard for his indecisive answer on the fate of the Princes.

R. G. MOULTON OF ALL SHAKESPEARE'S CRITICS

R. G. Moulton Of All Shakespeare's Critics has presented the revenge **theme** most forcefully. This holds in the great Shakespearean revival at the turn of the twentieth century, even when the play was again altered by the actor Richard Mansfield. He retained the spiritual conflict over avenging conscience. This revision by Mansfield (actually a revision of Cibber's text) is of interest because he tampered with such famous passages as Richard's opening soliloquy. After the lines, "And hate the idle pleasures of these days," Mansfield added, from Act III, sc. 2, pt. 3 of *Henry VI*: "Then, since this earth affords no joy to me," and the following six lines. In Mansfield's Nota prefixed to the published version of the play, he considers Richard has been rudely depicted by historians. More, Hall, and Holinshed are at greatest fault. He found it necessary to change the last act of the tragedy, "notably Richard's evil dream and the fight of Bosworth Field in which the actor has hoped to produce a greater realistic effect by following the tale of history." For each change Mansfield has an explanation: "Moreover, the great poet, in arranging the principal events of Gloster's life for dramatic treatment has so distorted, confused, and conglomerated deeds and events that it is most difficult to restore their sequence in the play or to follow history while we follow Shakespeare."

CHRISTOPHER MARLOWE

Christopher Marlowe has been considered the author of certain of Shakespeare's works, in part at least. *Richard The Third* is, according to J. M. Robertson, a reworking by Shakespeare of the anonymous *The True Tragedie of Richard III* earlier adapted by Marlowe. Mr. Robertson declares, "The psychology - the crude vaunt of villainy and terror stricken avowal of guilt - is that of Marlowe's unsubtle monster." He insists that the play "is a melodrama, not Shakespearean tragedy."

A. L. ROWSE IN A RECENT COMMENTARY

A. L. Rowse In A Recent Commentary on the play agrees that *King Richard The Third* is "Shakespeare's grand tribute to Marlowe." The play centers around a single character, the same as in Marlowe's *Tamburlaine* and *Dr. Faustus*, but there is a great difference. Here, he agrees with Richard Moulton when he says, "With this play history tends to pass . . . into tragedy." Perhaps P. Alexander has best summed up the story of Richard, noting that as it becomes "less of a fateful pageant and more the adventure of an individual soul."

RICHARD III

ESSAY QUESTIONS AND ANSWERS

Question: Discuss the concept of tragedy in *King Richard The Third*. Is it medieval or Renaissance?

Answer: To answer this question it is necessary to understand how the medieval writer defined tragedy. In Chaucer's *Prologue to the Monk's Tale,* he says, in substance, that tragedy is the story of one who stands in great prosperity, then in great sorrow falls from his high place and ends wretchedly. This rather direct approach became the pattern for the biographies of the kings and nobles who met wretched deaths in *The Mirror For Magistrates*. During the English renaissance something of the Greek poets' concept of tragedy was imposed on the medieval idea. More than that, it prompted the beginning of tragic drama in England. For the medievalist, God (though Fortune is often named) is the avenger for misdeeds. The Greek poets saw man's life as being beyond his control either by reason or by justice. Human beings impelled by an inner force do wrong, they argued, despite their good inclinations. Conscience is a distinctly medieval concept.

Richard's character is medieval in that he knows right from wrong and is capable through free will to choose either. He understands the power of conscience. But Shakespeare for a heightened ending buries it under a wealth of energy and his determined gaiety in being a villain. However, after the "ghost" scene, conscience creeps out and speaks to him with a "thousand several tongues." It accuses him of murder and perjury. In *King Richard The Third* we miss the soul searching that is such an integral part of *Hamlet* and the later tragedies. For this reason it is possible to underestimate the worth of Shakespeare's early artistry.

Question: In *King Richard The Third* has Shakespeare crowded the play with minor characters in order to emphasize Richard as a Marlovian type of figure?

Answer: In a particular sense no character in Shakespeare's plays just "fills in." Be it ever so small a role, each character has a definite moment in the play. As the net of Nemesis entangles each character in *King Richard The Third,* it would seem almost impossible that a dramatist could arrange for a Page, a groom, or a churchman to say or do a thing that is of vital importance to the action of the play. Sir Thomas Vaughan speaks only one line. With the Queen's brother, Rivers, and her son, Grey, Vaughan is executed unjustly by Richard. His single statement, "You live that shall cry woe for this hereafter," is the first pointer at retributive justice that will eventually overtake Richard. Another of the minor characters is John Morton, Bishop of Ely. In the play the Bishop has two tasks and they are seemingly minor: 1. He sits at the Council table with Richard and listens while the latter toys with the gullible Hastings, like a cat relishing a mouse, then beheads him for treason. What treason? Hastings will not agree to set aside the son of Edward IV as heir to the throne. The Bishop is silent, and does not appear again in the play. 2. When Richard is threatened by the army led by the young Duke of Richmond, word comes that the Bishop has "fled" to his aid. Richard comments, "Ely with Richmond troubles me" very deeply. As a churchman, the Bishop disapproves of tyrants. In Richard he sees one. His move plays an important part in Richard's defeat. These are only two examples, but more can be found that show the pains that Shakespeare took in complementing the minute details of plot and characterization.

Question: Is there any **imagery** in this early play that is comparable to that in Shakespeare's later plays?

Answer: While the **imagery** may not be comparable to that, say, in *Hamlet* or *Lear*, it approximates it many times. Richard's opening soliloquy is a delightful **metaphor**, "Now is the winter of our discontent." With a kind of jolly ease he goes on to sketch himself. He is not "shaped for sportive tricks"; he is "not made to court an amorous looking-glass." Richard's deformity occasions some of the most brash and invective verse in the play, particularly from the women characters. They seem strangely unafraid of him. In their **similes** they exhaust natural lore. Richard is a "bottled spider," and "elvish marked." To announce his death, Richmond repeats the name Margaret has used in her curse, "the bloody dog is dead." In Clarence's dream the repetition of all he saw at the bottom of the sea has elements of the lovely **imagery** found in *the Tempest*: "Inestimable stones, unvalued jewels," he saw them in "men's skulls: and, in those holes/ Where eyes did once inhabit, there were crept,/ As't were in scorn of eyes, reflecting gems." Again in this play Shakespeare has lessened the impact of imminent tragedy by diverting the attention to the charm of externals. The **imagery** is particularly appealing when the Queen stops to look back at the Tower where her children, who she instinctively knows will be victims of Richard's ruthless climb to power, are imprisoned. She begs the Tower to "pity" her young sons. Stones make a "rough cradle for such pretty ones." Sentimental as it may be, her caution to the Tower as "rude ragged nurse, old sullen playfellow," to use her "babies well," deepens the character of the Queen. **Imagery** for Shakespeare was a means to an end. With it he could make his lines purr, glow, or tremble at will.

Question: As one of the important Court nobles, what is the function of Buckingham in the play?

Answer: Buckingham appears in the play for the first time when King Edward IV brings his nobles together in an attempt to create a friendly alliance. It is then that Buckingham shows himself somewhat of a hypocrite. He tries always to be on the winning side. His allegiance at this time is wholly to Edward IV, who is gravely ill, but still the King. At the meeting, Buckingham feigns affection for the Queen and gives extravagant pledges of friendship. He even begs God to punish him if he fails to keep his pledge. His glib way pleases the King, and Buckingham has established himself. His first outward show of duplicity is his willingness to go with Richard "to comfort" the King, distraught over learning of Clarence's death despite his countermand of the warrant. But it is impossible to be a close associate of Richard and not agree completely with what he says and does.

Recognizing that wealth and advancement at Court are Buckingham's aims, Richard encourages him. He can be very useful in his climb to the throne. So it is not idle chatter when Richard flatters him, calling him his "oracle," and "prophet" and his "dear cousin." Then follow promises of an earldom and gifts. Believing himself Richard's alter ego, Buckingham delights in displaying his new powers. And he is so successful in ensnaring Hastings and then handling the London mob that Richard thinks it well to test his loyalty. Just how far in crime is Buckingham willing to go? Will he agree to the murder of the young Princes? His hesitation serves as Richard's answer. He sees some shreds of conscience left in Buckingham, so he can be of no more use to him.

In the final analysis Buckingham is rather a weak man than a completely evil one. He is willing to connive and plunder, but at the crucial moment he halts, remembering an oath, even though he had made it in jest, to be true to the children of Edward IV. Coldly turned out of Richard's Court, Buckingham asks himself, "Made I him King for this?"

Question: What evidence of the divine right of kings is there in *King Richard III*?

Answer: Critics have said that this is "a very religious play." The statement can be understood to mean that *Richard III* is "religious" in that Shakespeare uses the renaissance concept of religion as a motivating force. Divine right of kings is a religious concept that was firmly held by the Plantagenets and the Tudors who ruled England. While this doctrine is bound up with Fortune and her fickle ways, the only concern here is to what extent the two rulers, Richard and Richmond, feel themselves God's appointed agents. When Richard finally comes to the throne, he arrives convinced he is destined to rule. He surrounds himself with the protective aura of divine right. His right to rule is unassailable. When Edward's Queen and his mother, Duchess of York, try to thwart him, he orders his train, "Strike alarum, drums! Let not the heavens hear these tell-tale women/ Rail on the Lord's anointed. Strike, I say."

There is much the same attitude toward divine right in Richmond's prayer before the battle. His prayer is not said in Richard's haughty manner. Richmond addresses the Deity, "O Thou, whose captain I account myself/Look on my forces with a gracious eye." And he has scarcely finished the prayer when the ghosts, Richard's victims, come, promising him victory. There is an element of the morality play in the use of the ghosts as agents to point out the good and evil of a situation. It became a favorite device of the renaissance.

To justify Richmond's determination to dethrone Richard as an usurper, and the attitude of those nobles, such as Stanley, who fought against a supposed divinely appointed king, Shakespeare clarifies the lawfulness of fighting against an usurper and, in this case, a murderer as well. Richmond argues the point in addressing his troops: Richard "has ever been Go 's enemy./ God will in justice ward you as his soldiers." They will have put down a "tyrant" and can rest. And in placing Richard's crown on Richmond, Stanley refers to it as "this long-usurped royalty."

The idea that God permits rather than appoints kings to rule is never hinted at in the play. Richmond is certain that the Houses of York and Lancaster will not (through the marriage of Princess Elizabeth and Richmond) "By God's fair ordinance conjoin together."

Question: Is murder seemingly regarded less of a crime by the ruling class and nobility than by other citizens at the time of *Richard III?*

Answer: When Richard, Duke of Gloucester, declares that he is 'determined to prove a villain," it is equivalent to saying that he has killed conscience. For him, murder like all crime is a tool, and the best if one knows how to use it. The nobles at Court who have dabbled in crime with him are not as adept as he. When he engages the murderers to kill his brother, Duke of Clarence, he welcomes them as "stout resolved mates." His greeting implies that they too have smothered their consciences. The directives he gives them are purposely short and simple: be "obdurate" and "act swiftly." A few minutes before they arrive, he is almost gleeful over the way his twirling around "odd ends" from Scripture has helped him kill conscience. In Court circles he finds it easy to pass for a saint by quoting ever so piously that God commands one to do good for evil. Who at Court knows good from evil? So it is easy for him to pass off evil for good, or as he puts it, "seem a saint, when I most play the devil."

Of the two murderers involved in the killing of the Duke of Clarence, the Second is likely more cultured than his companion. But each displays some uneasiness over the deed. They become involved in a discussion over conscience and guilt. The Second Murderer becomes passive about the murder at hand when his companion remarks that their victim "shall never wake till the judgment day." The word "judgment" disturbs him. Though they have a warrant to kill and cannot be held guilty of murder, yet both can "be damned for killing him from which no warrant can defend" them. Dregs of conscience begin to bother him. But to the First Murderer, crime is merely a job which they both agreed to do, and they should get on with it.

The scene of the murder of the Duke of Clarence is a study in the power that conscience has to stir the mind. Acting contrary to the Duke of Gloucester's advice, the Second Murderer has led conscience weaken his resolve. He goes so far as to argue with his victim why he should not be killed. Finally, when the Duke warns, "He that set you on/ To do this deed will hate you for it," it becomes a choice between greed and conscience, and conscience wins. Though he is present, the Second Murderer takes no part in the actual crime.

The murder of the young Princes is an example of remorse of conscience. It affords a striking contrast between Tyrell, who oversees the murder, and Richard, who orders it. When he leaves the King, Tyrell is full of enthusiasm for the task. But a few hours after the murder, remorse of conscience overcomes him, and he is completely at its mercy. While he paces back and forth in a palace room waiting to make his report to the King, he sees the latter now as a "bloody king," and the murder is "the most arch-act of piteous massacre/ That ever yet this land was guilty of." As the full impact of the murder stirs him, he remembers each detail of it and the exact words of the men he hired to do it. Conscience and remorse so gnawed at them, that they left after briefly describing the murder and were unable to speak more.

Completely callous to emotion and brazen in crime, Richard asks Tyrell if he saw the children dead and buried. Assured that he did, the King will wait for a full account of the murder and go dine in peace! But despotic and tyrannical as he is, Richard comes finally to realize that his conscience was dormant, not dead. After the "dream" it is aroused and starts devouring him. To be rid of it, he would have to take "revenge" on himself. Suicide? He is afraid. This final soliloquy has in it inklings of Hamlet, but here there is no nobleness of spirit. It is rather the display of a mind reaping the agony and bitterness that it created.

Each of the nobles-Rivers, Grey, Hastings, and Buckingham-whom Richard sends to the scaffold has been in some way involved in murder. For each of them, as for Richard III, the end justifies the means. And each of them admits his guilt, as he does, when death comes. But none except the Second Murderer and Tyrell regard murder for what it is, namely, an offense against God. And only these two show any contrition for their offense; the rest fear His punishment.

STUDY REVIEW QUESTIONS

1. What villainous scheme does Richard III reveal in the opening soliloquy of the play?

2. Are Queen Margaret's curses on Richard III and others based on political or personal enmity?

3. Why does Lady Anne revile Richard when he proposes marriage to her?

4. Queen Elizabeth dislikes Richard and the Duke of Clarence, the brothers of her husband, King Edward IV. Why?

KING RICHARD THE THIRD

5. Why does the Second Murderer fail to keep his word to aid in the murder of the Duke of Clarence?

6. King Edward IV calls a meeting of the nobles of his Court. Why is the meeting called?

7. (a) What dire news is divulged at this meeting?
   (b) Why is it important to the nation?

8. Contrast the attitude of the Duchess of York toward her son, Richard III, in Act II, sc. 2, with that in Act IV, sc. 4.

9. How do the three Citizens of London react to the death of King Edward IV?

10. What are the differences of personality in the young sons of Edward IV as they chat with their Uncle Richard?

11. What is the burden of Catesby's message from Richard to Lord Hastings? What particular bearing does his answer have on the action of the play?

12. Who calls Pomfret Castle a "bloody prison"? Why?

13. What are the charges of treason that Richard brings against Hastings? What persons at the Court does he also involve?

14. What is the reaction of the Scrivener to the execution of Hastings?

15. How does Richard explain the mock "attack" on him and Buckingham to the Lord Mayor? What does he say in praise of Hastings? Do these remarks give insight into Richard's character.

16. Relative to his desire to be King, what definite instructions does Richard give Buckingham to relay to the Lord Mayor and the citizens?

17. How does Buckingham contrive to impress the crowd with Richard's piety and goodness?

18. After Buckingham's aid in making Richard King, why is he discarded by him?

19. What are the salient points of difference in the dialogues of the Two Murderers who killed Clarence in Act I, sc. 4, and in the soliloquy of Tyrell, who reports the details

of the murder of the Princes in the Tower? Are these differences moral, psychological, or social? Explain.

20. (a) Why does Richard think it important to his cause that he marry his brother's daughter?
    (b) What arguments can be given to show that Queen Elizabeth was feigning when she promised Richard that she would urge her daughter to marry him?

21. What two important decisions in the play are made by Stanley? How does each decision contribute to Richard's downfall?

22. What insight into Richard's character does his soliloquy give after the appearance of the ghosts? What does he say that would show retributive justice for his crimes?

23. In his address to his troops, before the battle of Bosworth Field, how does Richmond arouse their patriotism?

24. Explain how Stanley's delivery of his troops to his stepson at the crucial hour of the battle can be considered an act of loyalty rather than treason to the English nation.

25. What particular traits of character necessary for a good ruler are displayed in Richmond's address to his nobles and troops after his victory in battle? How does he announce his coming wedding to Elizabeth, daughter of Queen Elizabeth and King Edward IV?

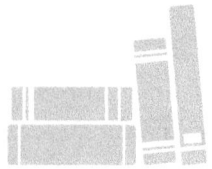

BIBLIOGRAPHY AND SUGGESTIONS FOR RESEARCH PAPERS

SHAKESPEARE'S SOURCES FOR KING RICHARD THE THIRD

Questions To Consider: What differences of characterization are there in the anonymous True *Tragedy of Richard III* and Shakespeare's play? As sources, do More and Holinshed agree?

Boas, F. S., *Christopher Marlowe*, London, 1939. Boas limits Shakespeare's debt to Marlowe.

Brooke, N., "Marlowe as Provocative Agent in Shakespeare's Early Plays," *Shakespeare Survey*, 30 ff.

Capra, Carlo, Il *Riccardo III* di Shakespeare e il *Mirror for Magistrates*," *English Miscellany*, xiii, 1962.

Carnall, Geoffrey, "Shakespeare's *Richard III* and St. Paul," *Shakespeare Quarterly*, xiv. Study of the possible influence of St. Paul on Shakespeare's conception of *Richard III*. Comment on his favorite oath, "By holy Paul."

Dover, Wilson J., "Malone and the Upstart Crow," *Shakespeare Survey* 4, 56 ff. Evaluates the justice of Green's accusations.

Driver, T. F., *The Sense of History In Greek and Shakespearean Drama*, New York, 1961. Contrasts of ancient and renaissance values in personalities and situations.

Farnham, Willard, "The Progeny of *A Mirror for Magistrates*," *Modern Phil.* xxix, 1932. Shakespeare's debt to the *Mirror* for *Richard III*.

Greer, A. C., "The Relation of Richard III to the True Tragedy of Richard, Duke of York," *Studies in Philology*, xlvii, 1932. Excellent comparative study of the two plays.

Harrison, G. B., "Shakespeare's Religion," *Commonweal*, July 2, 1948. An attempt to determine Shakespeare's religious views from his basic theological concepts in the plays. Also, interesting comments on his quotes from Scripture and use of oaths such as, "By our Lady," "By the Holy Rood," and "Have mercy, Jesu."

Kalson, A. E., "The Chronicles in Cibber's *Richard III*," *Studies in English Literature*, III.

Nugent, E. M., *Thought and Culture of the English Renaissance* 1481-1550), Cambridge, 1956. Contains More's *History of Richard III*.

Wilson, F. P., *Marlowe and the Early Shakespeare*, London, 1953.

KING RICHARD III AND NEMESIS

Questions To Consider: How closely does Shakespeare follow the Senecan pattern of revenge? Does Shakespeare in the character of Richard satirize or uphold conscience?

Alexander, P., *Shakespeare's Henry VI and Richard III*, New York, 1929. An excellent comparative study of the weakness and strength of these two kings.

Anderson, Ruth L., "The Pattern of Behavior Culminating in *Macbeth*," *Studies in English Literature*, III. Emphasizes *King Richard III*.

Campbell, L. B., "Theories of Revenge in Renaissance England," *Modern Philology*, xxviii, 1931. In her article Prof. Campbell presents a thorough study of the revenge scheme in its pagan, Judeo, and Christian concepts.

Shakespeare's Tragic Heroes, New York, 1952. The subtitle of this work is "Conceptions of History and Tragedy in *A Mirror For Magistrates*."

To Prove a Villain, "The Case of King Richard III," edited by Taylor Littleton and Robert R. Rea, New York, 1964. Prime source material and selections from critical studies of the play.

RICHARD III

GENERAL BIOGRAPHY AND CRITICISM

Alexander, P., *Shakespeare's Life and Art*, New York, 1961. Development of Shakespeare from apprentice to mature artist.

Brooks, C., "Shakespeare as a symbolist poet," *Yale Rev.*, June, 1945.

Chambers, E. K., *The Elizabethan Stage*, Oxford, 1923. A classic for the study of Shakespeare's stage problems.

Coleridge, S. T., *Shakespearean Criticism*, reprint, New York, 1961. An interesting study of the play from a nineteenth century critic's viewpoint.

Farnham, Willard, *Medieval Heritage of Elizabethan Tragedy*, New York, 1956. One of the most complete studies of the classical vs. medieval concept of tragedy. Excellent comments on *King Richard III.*

Goddard, Harold, *The Meaning of Shakespeare*, New York.

Green, V. H. H., *The Later Plantagenets*, London, 1955. Shows the weakness of the line that accounts for their fall from power.

Hazlitt, Wm., *Characters of Shakespeare's Plays*, modern reprint. Thinks *King Richard III* is better on the stage than read in quiet, as was then being urged by some.

Hughes, A. E., *Shakespeare and His Welsh Characters*. Interesting comments on the Duke of Richmond and his Welsh background.

Perry, Alice I., *Stage History of Shakespeare's King Richard The Third*, New York, 1909. This work gives a full account of the various acting editions of the play.

Rowse, A. L., *William Shakespeare*, New York, 1963. Gives an excellent re-evaluation of the critics' views on *King Richard III*.

Sprague, A. C., *Shakespearean Players and Performances*, Cambridge, 1954. An account of the late sixteenth century stage.

GENERAL: CLASSIC CRITICISM AND INTERPRETATION

Bradley, A. C. "Shakespeare's *Antony and Cleopatra*" in *Oxford Lectures on Poetry*. London, 1950.

Case, R. H. and M. R. Ridley. *Introduction to the Arden edition of Antony and Cleopatra*. Cambridge, Mass., 1955.

Chambers, E. K. *Shakespeare: A Survey*. London, 1925.

Charney, Maurice. *Shakespeare's Roman Plays*. Cambridge, Mass., 1961.

Coleridge, S. T. *Notes and Lectures upon Shakespeare*. London, 1849, V. I, 145-148.

Danby, John F. *Poets on Fortune's Hill*. London, 1952.

Dickey, Franklin M. *Not Wisely, But Too Well*. San Marino, Calif., 1957.

Dowden, Edward. *Shakespeare*. N. Y., 1881.

Dryden, John. *Preface to All for Love in Mermaid Series*. London, 1949-50

Farnham, Willard. *Shakespeare's Tragic Frontier*. Berkeley, Calif., 1950.

Granville-Barker, Harley. *Prefaces to Shakespeare*. Princeton, N. J., 1952, V. I.

Hazlitt, William. *Characters of Shakespeare's Plays*. London, 1957.

Holzknecht, Karl J. *The Background of Shakespeare's Plays*. N. Y., 1950.

Johnson, Samuel. *Samuel Johnson on Shakespeare* (ed. W. K. Wimsatt, Jr.). N. Y., 1960.

Knight, G. Wilson. *The Imperial **Theme***. London, 1951.

Knights, Lionel C. *Some Shakespearean Themes*. Stanford, Calif., 1960.

Mac Callum, M. W. *Shakespeare's Roman Plays*. London, 1910.

Mack, Maynard. *Introduction to the Pelican edition of Antony and Cleopatra*. Baltimore, 1960.

Ribner, Irving. *Patterns in Shakespearean Tragedy*. N. Y., 1960.

Rosen, William. *Shakespeare and the Craft of Tragedy*. Cambridge, Mass., 1960.

Spencer, T. J. B. *Shakespeare: The Roman Plays*. London, 1963.

Spurgeon, Caroline. *Shakespeare's **Imagery***. Boston, 1958.

Symons, Arthur. "*Antony and Cleopatra*," in *Studies in the Elizabethan Drama*. London, 1920.

Traversi, D. A. *Approach to Shakespeare*. London, 1938.

Van Doren, Mark. *Shakespeare*, N. Y., 1939.

Wilson, Harold S. *On the Design of Shakespearean Tragedy*. Toronto, 1957.

READINGS IN CRITICAL METHODS AS APPLIED TO SHAKESPEARE

Auerbach, Erich, *Mimesis* (1953), Ch. 13, "The Weary Prince" (Prince Hal in *Henry IV*, Part Two).

Brooks, Cleanth, *The Well-Wrought Urn* (1947), Ch. 2, "The Naked Babe and the Cloak of Manliness," (a study of **imagery** in *Macbeth*).

Downer, Alan S., "The Life of Our Design: The Function of **Imagery** in the Poetic Drama," in *Shakespeare: Modern Essays in Criticism*, ed. Leonard Dean (1957).

Empson, William, *The Structure of Complex Words* (1951), chapters on "Fool in *Lear*," and "Honest in *Othello*."

Fergusson, Francis, *The Human Image in Dramatic Literature* (1957), Part II, "Shakespeare."

___*The Idea of a Theatre* (1949), Ch. 4, "'*Hamlet*, Prince of Denmark;' The Analogy of Action."

Granville-Barker, *Harley On Dramatic Method* (1956), Ch. 3, "Shakespeare's Progress."

Kitto, H. D. F., *Form and Meaning in Drama* (1956), Ch. 9 "*Hamlet*."

LIFE AND TIMES OF SHAKESPEARE

Chute, Marchette. *Shakespeare of London.* New York, 1956. A very interesting biography that also provides analysis of Shakespeare's world.

Halliday, F. E. *Shakespeare: A Pictorial Biography.* New York, 1956. Excellent pictures.

Fluchere, Henri. *Shakespeare and the Elizabethans.* New York, 1956. Relates Shakespeare to the other dramatists of his time and to the world in which they lived.

Spencer, Theodore. *Shakespeare and the Nature of Men.* New York, 1951. A discussion of the philosophical background of Shakespeare's England with particular emphasis on man's place in nature.

Trevelyan, G. M. *History of England, Volume II: The Tudors and the Stuart Era.* New York, 1953. A good account of the history of Tudor England.

Tillyard, E. M. *The Elizabethan World Picture.* New York, 1944. An excellent description of the concepts, attitudes, and manners in Shakespearean England, supplying important background material for the understanding of all Shakespeare's work.

SHAKESPEAREAN THEATER PRODUCTION

Adams, John Cranford. *The Globe Playhouse: Its Design and Equipment.* New York, 1942.

De Banke, Cecile. *Shakespearean Production, Then and Now. A Manual for the Scholar Player.* New York, 1953.

Hodges, C. Walter. *The Globe Restored*. New York, 1954.

Smith, Irwin. *Shakespeare's Globe Playhouse. A Modern Reconstruction in Text and Scale* Drawings. New York, 1956.

These books describe the ways in which Shakespeare's plays were originally produced, and De Banke's account includes helpful suggestions for the modern producer.

SHAKESPEARE'S HISTORY PLAYS

Campbell, Lily B. *Shakespeare's Histories: Mirrors of Elizabethan Policy.* San Marino, California, 1947. An excellent description of the development of historiography in the English Renaissance, with a separate chapter on *Henry V* analyzed as the ideal victorious king.

Chambers E. K. *Shakespeares A Survey.* New York, 1959. A collection of essays on various Shakespeare plays, including an excellent chapter on *Henry V* in relation to patriotism in sixteenth century England.

Holzknecht, Karl J. *The Backgrounds of Shakespeare's Plays.* New York, 1950. A particularly useful account of the role of chroniclers and writers of popular history works for the theater in Tudor England. Shakespeare is seen in perspective with other men also concerned with historical themes.

Schelling, R. E. *The English Chronicle Play.* New York, 1902. An interesting discussion of the **genre** of the chronicle play flourishing before and during Shakespeare's lifetime.

Tillyard, E. M. W. *Shakespeare's History Plays*. London, 1956. An analysis of the myth of the Tudor Monarchy and the men who celebrated it in chronicle and drama, including Shakespeare. There is an excellent chapter on *Henry V* in this connection.

Traversi, Derek. *From Richard II to Henry V* Stanford, California, 1957. An exploration of the dominant **themes** in Shakespeare's **epic** of English history, with an interesting chapter emphasizing the moral development of the character of Henry V.

www.ingramcontent.com/pod-product-compliance
Lightning Source LLC
LaVergne TN
LVHW011714060526
838200LV00051B/2906